LEARNING TO SHARE

VOLUME-TWO

About the Editors

This book has been edited by **Dr. Neela Mukherjee** and **Dr. Bratindi Jena** on behalf of the SRIJ group on participatory development, which is an informal and a non-funded group of professionals involved in such activities. The SRIJ groups cuts across different disciplines, organizations and work areas.

Dr. Neela Mukherjee is currently a development consultant to multiple organizations, action researcher, teacher and a trainer. Formerly, a Professor of Economics at the LBS National Academy of Administration Mussoorie, Dr. Mukherjee's research interests are topical and varied. An alumna of the London School of Economics and Political Science, her major areas of current research includes participatory development, participatory methods, community perspectives and environment and trade-related issues.

Dr. Bratindi Jena, currently employed as a Programme officer at Action Aid India, is responsible for planning and implementation of projects in North Bihar. Earlier, she worked as a research officer at IDS, Jaipur on a research project on livelihood adaptation: gender, civil society and public action. She obtained her Ph.D. in Psychology from Delhi University in 1995 and was also a visiting fellow in the autumn of 1997, at the Institute of Development Studies at Sussex, UK.

LEARNING TO SHARE

Experiences and Reflections on PRA and Other Participatory Approaches

VOLUME-TWO

Edited by

NEELA MUKHERJEE
BRATINDI JENA

CONCEPT PUBLISHING COMPANY, NEW DELHI-110059

ISBN 81-7022-864-6 (Vol. 2)

ISBN 81-7022-663-5 (Series)

First Published 2001

Published and Printed by
Ashok Kumar Mittal
Concept Publishing Company
A/15-16, Commercial Block, Mohan Garden
NEW DELHI-110059 (India)

Phones : 5648039, 5649024
Fax : 091-11-5648053
E-mail: publishing@conceptpub.com

EDITORIAL

The present edited volume is a collection of papers, which is a sequel to Volume One of the series 'Learning to Share', published in 1997 by the Concept Publishing Company. The first volume of 'Learning to Share' was based on our presumption that there is a need for documenting and sharing of PRA-type field experience from time to time. There are many PRA-type activities and innovative processes taking place in the field of participatory development though opportunities for sharing such experience stand limited. It was for this reason that in 1997, a group of development pactitioners worked as a team to document their field experience and publish their notes and papers as a collected volume. One main objective was sharing of such experience with those involved/ interested in similar activities. This is how the first volume of 'Learning to Share' got published. The Participatory Group of the Institute of Development Studies at the University of Sussex supported the volume by making arrangements for its distribution to PRA Networks across the globe.

The positive response received for the Volume One of 'Learning to Share' validated our feeling that documenting and sharing of experience are important activities as means of mutual learning. Based on such enthusiastic response, received on Volume One of 'Learning to Share', we thought that editing another volume would be a fruitful effort in terms of sharing subsequent field experience and that is how the present volume has emerged. The contributors of the papers and notes for the present volume are development practitioners associated with participatory development. Since 'practitioner' is a generic term it is important to mention that such contributors are field-based practitioners, where most of them are also engaged in Participatory Action Research (PAR). They are involved in field-based processes and methods in PRA-type approaches in different areas.

Participatory Research and Conventional Academic Research

Since the papers in this volume are the outputs of 'participatory research' and not conventional 'academic research' it is important, at the outset, to distinguish between the two kinds of research. The two sets of researchers 'academic' and those engaged in 'participatory action' are two distinct categories in terms of their nature of research, orientation and the research tools used. Though there exists common ground between the two categories of researchers in terms of research analysis, there are basic differences between them in approach, orientation and methods.

While, distinguishing academic research from PAR it is important to point out that academic research is rooted in theory and such theoretical hypotheses are tested on the basis of empirical research to see how they work. In contrast, PAR is field-based and originates from the field where such research is grounded in field realities. It may or may not have theoretical backup. In certain situations it can also lead to emergence of theoretical framework based on empirical underprinnings, thereby enriching theory. As pointed out by Chambers (1997) there is contrast between practicing and academic professions. They differ in the value they place on practice and theory. The practicing professions are concerned more with action, the academics more with understanding.

While the approach in PAR is to listen and learn from the people and augment such research process through further action, academic research can be entirely theoretical or empirical/applied research based on processed/semi-processed data. In terms of orientation, PAR adopts a learning mode and is based on open-ended field inquiry while academic research is more 'close-ended', 'controlled' and 'structured' in terms of objectives, hypotheses and analysis. Applied academic research is mostly based on secondary data collected by means of questionnaire survey while participatory research is based on field-oriented processes and methods.

The quantitative bias in academic research is very much a part of the methods used and the kind of orientation/discipline, which an academic researcher has. This is quite different from the qualitative and process-oriented emphasis of PAR. In this context, Chambers (1997) writes that conventional/normal professionalism creates and sustains its own reality, where the professional methods and values set a trap. The "reductionist, controlled, simplified and quantified construction" becomes 'reality' for isolated academic professionals. The ways of validation of the two kinds of research are quite at variance. The academic research has more to do with accuracy and 'representativeness' of data while participatory research has more in terms of validation by people (Mukherjee, 1995).

Both PAR and academic research are valuable in their own way though for realistic and field-based analysis, the former has a definite advantage over the latter. In order to appreciate this point it is important to provide an overview of PAR and delve into its different aspects. PAR is not an ordinary combination of three words "Participatory," "Action" and "Research," rather it is a positive synergy built around a 'constructivist' approach based on objectives, methods and principles of participatory development. Such research is intrinsically field-based relating to any area within the broad contours of 'development'. It is not academic or laboratory research that is generally described as PAR though these can form components of PAR as parallel activities. Such research is strongly centered around grassroots participation. Conventionally academic research is thought to be of higher value. However, over the years PAR has assumed its own significance, meaning and value as a way of research, much of it being implicit in the ongoing ethos of field research in participatory development.

'Participation' in Action Research

Earlier, the term used was that of "action research" describing thereby those activities undertaken to meet development objectives and for augmenting professional knowledge. Now with the shift in the development paradigm towards "people's participation," the form and character of action research has also got transformed. It is being re-looked and re-organised for making it inherently "participatory" in character and hence, more relevant for meeting participant's needs. Though 'participation' can be of different kinds from passive participation of people to their active involvement, the emphasis is on the latter for meaningful participatory development. It is increasingly being observed that in the sphere of participatory development, process-based and value-based action research is considered superior in quality as compared to that research, which is not based on active participation and is relatively 'extractive', ad-hoc and more structured in nature.

Tracking the term "action research" over past years, we find that it has been variedly defined with/without emphasising the word 'participation'. While the definitions are varying, it is not difficult to find common denominators of such definitions. Moris and Copestake (1993) write that action research refers to those activities intended to achieve tangible development goals and at the same time which increase our understanding of how these goals can be achieved. As per this definition, action research is very much a piece of research with dual-objectives such as pursuing development activities and also finding out ways of improving upon them.

Action research by Kemmis and McTaggart (1982) is the linking of the terms 'action' and 'research' that highlights the essential feature of the method: trying out ideas in practice as a means of improvement and as a means of increasing knowledge. This definition implies that action research is a double-edged weapon for improving practice and increasing knowledge. Alternatively, according to Elliot (1991) action research is about improving practice rather than producing knowledge. So it is merely not for knowledge sake that action research is undertaken, it is rather for improving upon past practices where gain of knowledge comes as a corollary.

Lomax (1990) defined that action research is a way of defining and implementing relevant professional development. It starts small with a single committed person focusing on his/her practice. It gains momentum through the involvement of others as collaborators. As Lomax (1990) says that it can result in the formation of a self-critical community, extended professionals in the best sense of the term. While, McNiff, Lomax and Whitehead (1996) emphasized that action research involves many people other than the researcher, and the way in which these people are involved is crucial to such research. They also write that action research involves people and community and the methodology involved is very important.

From the above definitions of action research we can derive a list of important aspects of such research, which highlight both its narrow and broad spectrums. Action research, in narrow terms, is undertaken for improving upon past practices and increasing knowledge for achieving tangible development goals and/or relevant professional self-development. We also find a shifting stance of action research over time where participants' involvement is considered crucial. In its broader ambit, action research implies involvement of many people as collaborators and the methodology of such involvement is also a crucial part of such research. The dimension of 'participation' added to 'action research' not only enriches such research and enhances its value but also makes it more meaningful and broad-based. The angle of 'participation' helps in creating space for active involvement of those who normally participate in research activities, either as passive informants and whose contributions remain suppressed/extracted and hardly recognized. For any action research to become 'participatory' the following questions become relevant.

Some Relevant Questions

Who undertakes the PAR and with what purpose?
What is the process of such research and whose views get reflected?
Who participates in the research process and how?

Who owns the research process and how?
What impact it creates and who is benefited in the process?

From field experience one finds that such PAR is initiated either by 'insider' (the people) or by 'outsider' (practitioner) or by both collaborating as a team. The objectives can be varied for PAR and it is important to mention in this context that it is possible for an action researcher to engage in some form of self-development in addition to larger objectives. Another issue is whether the tools, techniques and process adopted for such research are participatory thereby creating enough space for the people to be actively involved in such research. It is important that poor, women, aged and the marginalized groups are included as participants apart from rest of the group/community. The more they 'own' the research process, the more they can influence the outcome and the greater is the degree of participation. So PAR is a broad spectrum where the degree of participation can range from one end to the spectrum to another depending on the way and objectives of involving people.

In PAR, it is also possible that the community is actively participating of its own choice and is setting the research agenda and the issues to be covered (White, 1999). The larger agenda for action research covers both insiders' and outsiders' agenda and has both direct and indirect impact on different levels of policy and practice. The research results are generally of relevance to the community but may or may not be practicable depending on the availability of resources. In absence of appropriate resources, it often leads to rising of community expectations (though not always) followed by inaction/disappointment. Hence, clarification of objective/s from the very start is an important component of PAR.

Another question, relevant to PAR is "how do we improve upon what we are doing?" The core of the research rests on "participatory action," which is in the driver's seat and such research informs practice. PAR is a powerful method in the hands of research facilitators and needs to be used with care so as not to become 'extractive'. It is desirable that it is undertaken in a manner so as to ensure the participation of the weak and the marginalized groups/communities and for making it light bearing and fruit bearing in practice. Increasingly, the 'vibes' from participatory field research provide a message that the challenge of PAR lies in not mere involvement of communities as passive objects of research but in their active involvement in the research process. It implies involvement of local communities in discussion and deliberation of research agenda, analysis of issues, ownership of processes and concomitant action.

Relevance of PAR

The next issue is related to the relevance and utility of PAR in the context of development. Some of the points are indicated below:

* Development activities are complex and decision-making is not a simple task. Often the forces determining development activities are too intricate and not easy to decipher. Generally speaking, there are no 'blueprints' available for participatory development and there is dearth of availability of definite answers or customized solutions to issues in such process. Hence, there are many 'empty boxes' in the sphere of participatory development, which PAR can help to answer for exploring possible ways of filling such boxes.
* It is important to have activities on a pilot basis and trial runs on a smaller scale before attempting activities on a larger plane. PAR as a part of any pilot project can provide clues for addressing unknown issues in the terrain of development activities. It helps in confidence building for undertaking new areas of activities/action and new challenges. Sometimes in order to influence policy-making and key decisions, results/evidence from PAR can be crucial. Based on such PAR, new policy parameters can be framed and implemented.
* PAR is useful in validating experimental and innovative efforts and creates base for 'scaling up' and replication of process. It helps in diagnostic analysis and in highlighting and verifying issues. It helps in better understanding and preparation for undertaking/sustaining project-related activities. It creates space for serving larger communities based on such experience.
* PAR is a way of focusing on selected issues and bringing about improvement in practice. It makes learning-by-doing possible. It helps in undertaking mid-way corrections and to improve upon process of individual/group learning. Such action research can lead to the formation of a self-critical community.

The full benefit of any action research can be generally realized through some form of systematic documentation, both qualitative and quantitative, which is not so common in practice.

About the Book

There is a plethora of field-based activities happening all around. Many of us are involved in innovative activities in the field with local communities. Though community participation can be vibrant and innovative it can also pose issues for which readymade answers seldom exists. It is in such cases that there is need for PAR to look more closely at some activity, process, theme, dimension, method, etc. Often it poses as a challenge for development workers to organize and facilitate such participation and also sustain it. The book gives us a glimpse of such activities in different areas and locations. The contributors are field practitioners, who have written on their field experience and/or have documented and analysed field results to identify the emerging trends. It is the micro-level pictures sketched by the authors, which is indicative of the larger picture of PRA-type activities happening in the field of participatory development.

The papers in this volume are not academic exercises, rather lessons shared from the field, real and happening. The notes and papers written by field practitioners are based on different locations across Andhra Pradesh, Himachal Pradesh, Rajasthan, Uttar Pradesh and West Bengal. The topics covered in this book include participatory eco-restoration, women's food calendar, participatory livestock development, participatory forestry, participatory village profile, bio-diversity monitoring, participatory need assessment, children's perceptions of livelihood and participatory impact assessment.

Contributions to this Volume

In her paper "Participatory Eco-Restoration—Breaking Grounds in Participatory Action Research," Jyotsna Sitling has described field experience from Doon Valley Watershed Management Project in the sphere of eco-restoration through local community initiative. And also sustaining and owning of such process by local community members. The paper provides detailed account of the process-oriented approach towards participatory eco-restoration based on *shramdan* (free labour) by village groups. The process of 'scaling up' of such community-initiated eco-restoration is also described in the paper. The paper describes in considerable detail how such approach was conceptualized, planned, acted upon, monitored and evaluated by village groups. The paper highlights the importance of participatory campaigning and brings to the fore the cumulative gains over time from each campaigning exercise, the challenges in involving the community and 'scaling' it up over a wider area, the monitoring and evaluation activities by the community and aspects of village networking.

Amitava Mukherjee and Neela Mukherjee's paper "Rural Women and Food Insecurity: What Food Calendars Reveal—A Longitudinal Study" is a study on food security in a tribal village of West Bengal based on 3 food calendars prepared by village women over time. Such seasonal food calendars constructed in 1993, 1995 and 1998 by women groups show trends in food insecurity, seasonal deficits of food, patterns of food consumption and the underlying forces influencing temporal access to food. The concept of food security described in the paper is an extension of Sen's entitlement and deprivation thesis. The paper highlights the knowledge of rural women in gathering food from the commons, forests and micro-environments; two, their role in such procurement; and three, the seasonality of food, its shortage and dependence on different sources. One major conclusion of the paper is the increase in hunger, over time, amongst the poor households. The loss of common property resources, in particular, have contributed towards stretching of hunger periods and robbing poor households of such a safety net provided by nature. Such increase in food insecurity in the village under study, in poverty pockets of rural India are not captured by macro indicators of National Food Security. One main suggestion by the authors are that at the policy level, poverty reduction schemes should be made more gender-sensitive so as to create space and scope for women managed projects for overcoming food insecurity.

In the paper "PRA and Livestock Development in India: The Emerging Scenario," Mahesh Chander and Sanjay Kumar make the point that the use of PRA methodology is limited in livestock sector and 'why' and 'how' PRA should be used for studying livestock situation. The paper deals with selected issues relating to use of PRA for livestock development in the Indian context. The authors share some of their results from their recent research. The authors point out that the PRA methods help to explore the inter-relationship of livestock with farming system, housing system, feed and fodder availability, feeding strategies, care of young, etc. PRA methods help local livestock functionaries to understand local livestock management system. The authors also lists key uses of PRA in livestock sector development such as participatory livestock mapping, community livestock preferences, documentation of indigenous knowledge and practices, status of health, disease and nutrition and seasonal resource analysis for livestock, feed and fodder preferences and others. There is evidence of interest in PRA amongst research and training institutions including field veterinary practitioners. The paper establishes a case for applying PRA to livestock sector management in India. It states that PRA's across the country would help in framing a suitable and sustainable livestock development policy for the country.

In his note, "Evolving Process of People's Participation in Forestry: A Review of Experience in Rajasthan," Abhijit Ghose has traced the element of people's participation, which was gradually introduced in the activities of Forest Department of Rajasthan, India. The note shows how the paradigm shift was brought about in terms of actions in making people's participation, a field reality. The note describes how the 'role reversal' took place and the conventional objectives of the Forest Department were adjusted to match with people's priorities. Ghose also outlines the changes in the parameters of the forest policy of the Forest Department and how the concept of forest protection and management has progressed over time in terms of 'empowerment'. The Village Forest Protection and Management Committee (VFPMC) is empowered to do decision-making and execution of development activities, which reinforces its strength. The 'shift' in forest policy continues. Space for women's participation in VFPMC is also being created. The sharing formula for proceeds, between Forest Department and local communities, is being improved upon and 'entry point' activities are being looked upon as 'icebreakers' and ways of rapport building with local communities for initiating micro level development. The author is in favour of periodic review of the process of participation, to ensure adequate sensitization and clarity of understanding of the stockholders and strenthening of local level institutions.

Sudipta Ray has prepared "A Profile of Maraon: A Peri-Urban Village in Varanasi" based on participatory interactions for describing the significance of agriculture and livestock as a means of livelihood in an urbanized context. The village is located in the peri-urban areas, near the city of Varanasi and is exposed to the rapid impact of urbanization and industrialization in neighbouring areas. Ray visited village Maraon and undertook a wide range of discussions with the villagers in different hamlets. The range of topics covered were livelihood strategies of Maraon community, agriculture, livestock raising, seasonal activities, agricultural constraints, income, loans, farmers' innovations, crop rotations, changes in cropping patterns, quality of living, institutional set-up and benefits and costs of urbanization and industrialization. The village profile describes changes in farming systems over time, intensification of agricultural inputs and commercialization of agriculture, diversification of livelihood, fragility of the support system and the cost-benefit of rapid urbanization and industrialization.

Virinder Sharma's note on "PRA Workshop on Biodiversity Monitoring with Local Communities of Mehli in Himachal Pradesh" is based on a PRA monitoring workshop held at Mehli site during

September-October 1999. In his note he describes the objectives of the workshop, criteria for site selection, the way the workshop was conducted and the output. The workshop was interactive involving villagers and school children as participants. The villagers mapped and identified their natural and social resources and land use and also validated the scientists' findings. About grass, fauna and flora species, the villagers described such species, their characteristics features and trends. The villagers identified different local grass species along with their properties, quantity, quality and changing patterns. Two main outputs resulting from such workshop were a baseline on biodiversity and a monitoring register of Mehli consisting of status and changing patterns of fauna and flora.

In her paper "Rural Problem Prioritisation and PRA" Sumita Dawra has documented how PRA techniques were utilised for problems prioritized by rural women in the coastal district of Krishna in Andhra Pradesh, India. The rural women from different self-help groups in Krishna District were facilitated through PRA method for generation their own priority needs based on identification of their problems. For generating maximum participation of the target population and doing away with the planner's bias in leading the process, PRA methodology was utilized for problem prioritisation. There were 947 PRA exercises conducted in 726 villages in which problems were identified and ranked by poor women. For conducting such exercises 1631 local Anganwadi workers and 365 volunteers from women self-help groups were trained in PRA in 13 training camps spread over a total duration of 6 days. Such village-specific data received from 947 villages were computerized, village-wise, and their ranks and frequencies studied along with graphical presentation. A total of 54 problems were generated by the exercise, the eight most frequent major problems being latrines, ration cards, house sites, drinking water, pensions, drainage, roads and electricity. Of all the needs generated, need for toilets and drinking water were identified as problems of greatest magnitude based on the ranks allotted to them. Though these were not always identified across the villages with the same frequency. The paper provides background and analysis of the major problems highlighted by poor women. According to Dawra similar exercises and analysis from the grassroots can lead to focused areas of interventions by policy-makers, NGO's, donor agencies while formulating rural development programmes.

In her note "Children's Perceptions on Livelihood," Bratindi Jena documents results from PRA exercises involving children in a desert village of Sekhasar in Tehsil Phalodi of District Jodhpur, Rajasthan. The

PRA exercise with 6 boys and 5 girls in the age-group of 10 to 15 years was undertaken with the objective of learning about children's understanding of livelihood through their drawings. Such drawings on livelihood were followed by discussions. The results of such PRA exercise showed the children's gender bias in terms of livelihood and also the impact of conditioning on girls and boys and the different ways in which they grow up. The results also illustrate how children's views on livelihood were different from those of adults in the same village. Jena states that children have the capacity to express themselves in their own way through drawings and one needs to have patience and understanding for approaching them. If the children are given space by adults and are involved in development planning it can have a lasting impact on society. In such a case such planning would be more balanced on material and spiritual sides and create a healthy environment and a better world for the next generation. Jena concludes that in order to be sustainable any development programme must involve children.

In their paper "Participatory Impact Assessment—Land and Water Management in Movai Kalan Village of Mirzapur, Uttar Pradesh" V.Ch.S. Bahadur and Kripa Sankar have described participatory assessment of a lift irrigation project on the lives of Kol tribe residing in Movai Kalan village in Hallia block of District Mirzapur, Uttar Pradesh. The project objectives were multiple ranging from providing support to people's agricultural production through irrigation, reducing migration by increasing employment and income, improving conditions of women and demonstrating gains from community-based management of natural resources. The methodology adopted for impact assessment of the project was consultation with beneficiary groups and individuals using participatory tools and field visits. The paper documents how the participatory methods helped in learning about different aspects of the project impact. One major impact was through the participatory approach to project implementation, which helped in motivating the local groups to take over the project activities and manage their own natural resources, finance and instruments.

In this volume, we have tried to cover a large canvass of field experience on PAR, as shown above, relating to different topics in different locations. We acknowledge that there are shortcomings of this book for we know how difficult it is to capture 'field reality' in terms of a paper or a book. There can be many lapses in documenting field realities and different 'world views'. We are aware that field documentation is often, not that neat and tidy and suffer from the usual practitioner's bias. Admitting such imperfections/limitations and 'embracing errors' are important aspects of PAR. Howsoever, imperfect the papers are in this volume, we strongly believe that it is important to document and share our field experience. It is precisely for this reason that, we are engaged in a process of sharing such experience through different volumes and would like to continue with similar activity in future.

Without mentioning a long list of individual names, our sincere thanks are to all those who encouraged us to edit this series on "Learning to Share." We would also like to thank those who contributed papers to this volume. We express our heartiest thanks to Ashok Mittal of the Concept Publishing Company who has taken a keen interest in the publication of this series.

The amount received as royalty from the publication of Volume One "Learning to Share" was donated to Friendicoes, a Society in Delhi involved in eradication of cruelty to animals. We hope to do something similar with the royalty proceeds for the Volume Two.

The book is meant for all those who are interested and involved in the area of participatory development. We hope the readers find this book interesting and useful.

3 March 2000

Neela Mukherjee, New Delhi
and
Bratindi Jena, Patna

REFERENCES

Chambers, Robert (1997), *Whose Reality Counts?, Putting the First Last*, Intermediate Technology Publications, London.

Elliot, J. (1991), *Action Research for Educational Change*, Milton Keynes, Open University Press.

Kemmis, S. and McTaggart, R. (1982), *The Action Research Planner*, Australia, Deakin University Press.

Lomax, P. (1990), "An Action Research Approach to Development Staff in Schools" in P. Lomax (ed.), *Managing Staff Development in School*, Clevedon, Multi-Lingual Matters, 2-7.

McNiff, Jean, Pamela Lomax and Jack Whitehead (1996), *You and Your Action Research Project*, Routledge and Hyde Publications, London and New York.

Moris, Jon and James, Copestake (1993), *Qualitative Enquiry for Rural Development—A Review*, Intermediate Technology Publications, Overseas Development Institute.

Mukherjee, Neela (1997), *Participatory Rural Appraisal and Questionnaire Survey (Comparative Field Experience and Methodological Innovations)*, Concept Publishing Company, New Delhi.

White, Shirley A., ed. (1999), *The Art of Facilitating Participation, Releasing the Power of Grassroots Communication*, Sage Publications, London.

CONTENTS

CONTRIBUTOR'S PROFILE

Jyotsna Sitling

Jyotsna Sitling is from the Indian Forest Service, 1987 Batch. Presently working as Deputy Project Director Project Implementation in the Doon Valley Watershed Management Project in Rishikish. She has the experience of past twelve years in working with village communities of hills on participatory forest management. Over the past four and half years she has been actively involved in participatory action research for developing systems with the village communities of Garhwal hills on sustainable natural resource management. She has shared her grassroots experiences through lectures and presentations in various renowned institutions (Indira Gandhi National Forest Academy, Indian Institute of Management Ahmedabad and LBS National Academy of Administration, Mussoorie).

Amitava Mukherjee

Dr. Amitava Mukherjee is a noted economist and former Executive Director of ActionAid India, one of the largest international non-governmental funding organization in India. Dr. Mukherjee has written extensively on participation, rural development, food security and micro-level planning. He has 25 books and many papers on the above subject to his credit.

Neela Mukherjee

Dr. Neela Mukherjee currently a development consultant to multiple organizations, both in India and abroad. Formerly a Professor of Economics at Lal Bahadur Shastry National Academy of Administration, Mussoorie (Uttar Pradesh), India. Dr. Mukherjee's major area of research lies in participatory development in which she was written extensively. Her books include *Participatory Appraisal of Natural Resources* (1997), *Participatory Rural Appraisal: Methodology and Applications* (1993), and *Participatory Rural Appraisal and Questionnaire Survey*

(Comparative Field Experience and Methodological Innovations) (1995) published by Concept Publishing Company, New Delhi. Dr. Mukherjee has long experience of conducting training programmes for governmental, non-governmental and donor agencies in the areas of participatory rural appraisal, project sustainability, participatory monitoring and evaluation, participatory health need assessment etc.

Mahesh Chander

Dr. Mahesh Chander is an Agriculture graduate with post-graduate qualifications (M.Sc, Ph.D) in Agricultural extension education. He has been working with the Indian Council of Agricultural Research (ICAR) since 1991 as Agricultural Research Service Scientist in the discipline of Agricultural Extension. He is currently posted at Division of Extension Education, Indian Veterinary Research Institute, Izatnagar as Scientist (Senior Scale). As such, he is involved with post-graduate teaching, research, and field extension activities. His current interests include participatory extension activities for livestock development and organic farming. In his areas of his interest he has contributed many articles and presented papers in different conferences.

Sanjay Kumar

Sanjay Kumar is an Agricultural graduate with post-graduation in Dairy Economics from National Dairy Research Institute, Karnal. He is an Agricultural Research Service Scientist of Indian Council of Agricultural Research (ICAR) in the discipline of Agricultural Economics, currently posted at Mukteswar campus of Indian Veterinary Research Institute. He is engaged with livestock extension activities and research on livestock economics.

Abhijit Ghose

Abhijit Ghose, an officer of Indian Forest Service (1976) belongs to Rajasthan cadre. He held various posts in forest department of Rajasthan Government and now posted as Chief Conservator of Forests, IGNP, Bikaner. He also held the post of Joint Director (Administration) in National Forest Academy, Dehradun between 1991-95. His area of interests is in project formulation, research and training, computer applications in foresty and participatory forest management besides desert afforestation. He always likes to pilot innovative approaches in varied fields of his interest.

Sudipta Ray

Sudipta Ray is a senior research associate at Society for Development Studies, New Delhi. She has been engaged in studies on the impact of industrialisation on peri-urban communities and green lungs of the cities. Presently, she is working towards the promotion of sustainable livelihoods in the to-be resettled urban slums through policy analysis and community empowerment.

Virinder Sharma

Dr. Virinder Sharma is currently working as Principal Scientific Officer in the H.P. State Council for Science, Technology and Environment, Shimla. His Ph.D. involved extensive field studies on birds in Himachal Pradesh and intensive studies on Wildlife Biology. He has experience of research on the Himalayan Environment and is credited with significant work in the area of biodiversity, application of Participatory Rural Appraisal methods and environmental awareness. Presently, he is coordinating three International donor projects on environment, biodiversity and health (NORAD, AUSAID and EC).

He has to his credit one book on Himalayan Biodiversity and number of publications. He has visited several countries like England, Australia, Benelux, China and Pakistan to coordinate environmental studies. He is a member of various International and National Conservation Agencies. His current interest is in the participatory monitoring of natural resources through local communities.

Sumita Dawra

Sumita Dawra is an M.A., M.Phil. in Economics and MBA (Marketing and Finance), from Punjab University, Chandigarh. She belongs to 1991 batch of the Indian Administrative Service, Andhra Pradesh cadre. She has held postings of Sub-Collector, Rajahmundry (East Godavari District), Sub-Collector, Narsapur (West Godavari District), Chief Executive Officer, Zilla Parished, East Godavari District, Project Director, DRDA, Warangal District, Presently she is holding the post of Project Director, DRDA, Krishna district. She has a number of papers on rural development.

Bratindi Jena

Dr. Bratindi Jena, currently employed as a Programme officer at Action Aid India, is responsible for planning and implementation of projects in North Bihar. Earlier, she worked as a research officer at IDS, Jaipur on a research project on livelihood adaptation: gender, civil society and public action. She obtained her Ph.D. in Psychology from Delhi University in 1995 and was also a visiting fellow in the autumn of 1997, at the Institute of Development Studies at Sussex, UK.

V. Ch. S. Bahadur

V.Ch. S. Bahadur is a development worker and an expert in watershed management. He is associated with several development organizations.

Kripa Sankar

Kripa Sankar is an economist educationist. He is the Founder-Chairman of a well known grassroots development organization called Arthik Anusandhan Kendra, Mirzapur. He has written extensively on rural development.

LIST OF FIGURES

LIST OF TABLES

1

PARTICIPATORY ECO-RESTORATION
Breaking Grounds in Participatory Action Research

JYOTSNA SITLING

Background

In the Doon Valley Project, the overall responsibility of implementing community participation as envisaged by the project for meeting the overall objectives rests with the Field Deputy Project Directors (DPDs). Field DPDs are supported by technical staff of different disciplines from line departments and women motivators for this purpose. The author is one of the field DPDs posted at Rishikesh Division which covers the watershed area of about 40,000 hac comprising of seven micro-watersheds and is presently working with local communities of 63 villages located in the Garhwal hills.

This is a process documentation of an ongoing grassroot level action research taken up since the beginning of 1997 with the local communities in 63 villages of the Doon Valley watershed management project area for eco-restoration.

The systems development involved in two years of research exercise 1997-98 aims at transforming the advocacy for eco-restoration of the watershed area into the practical movement of the local communities. This research exercise involves exploring local perceived needs, local initiatives and local efforts of local communities in the context of their traditional socio-cultural values to combat their ecological problems. It tries to built upon them in a manner so that the villagers find their local initiatives and efforts rewarding to handle the problem of environmental degradation and for owning of responsibility to conserve it. The research exercise has laid emphasis on formation of strong village based forums for self-help where *Shramdan* (voluntary labour) has been used as a vital participatory tool. The tools for mass advocacy for eco-restoration has been particularly explored and used to target the attitudinal change of the members of the community from within. The focus has been mostly on evolving and adopting cheaper and effective ways of erosion controlling practices. This is mainly because the support which these village institutions would receive from the line agencies in future for erosion controlling measures will be grossly inadequate against the quantum of erosion taking place in these areas.

A PROFILE OF PEOPLE'S PARTICIPATION IN THE DOON VALLEY AREA FOR ECO-RESTORATION

The Issue

The effects of environmental degradation in the regions of Doon Valley are well-known. Human activities like overuse of forest resource, wrong farming practice, overgrazing by livestock, reckless mining and faulty land use have led to destruction of plant and tree cover thus exposing the earth to soil erosion, flood and scarcity of water leading to hardship, ultimately adversely effecting the quality of life of the inhabitants.

It is in this background that the Doon Valley Watershed Management Project is working with the local people for the eco-restoration of the region.

The Approach

The Project approach is to work hand in hand with the local people of the Doon Valley, taking up initiatives with them to bring into focus the reason for revival of their degraded environment in a community based integrated approach. Village institutions have become a platform of mutual learning for the Watershed Management Project personnel and the villagers. Here, the Project staff explore the unique socio-cultural environment of rural communities in relation to their innate understanding of their nature and natural resource by virtue of remaining in constant communion with it. At the same time they try to explore and understand many subtle and crucial factors that come to underplay in making a community indifferent to degraded environment. At this level the Project Staff interact and work with the collective consciousness of rural communities for the betterment of their degraded environment for the situation can improve if only the villagers own the responsibility to conserve it.

Drawing from the rich experience built on mutual confidence and learning as above, it was decided in the month of January 1997 that time had come to do some concrete work with local people for activating their support towards the objective of the Project, *i.e.*, the eco-restoration of the Doon Valley. But all the emphasis had to be laid on self-help to ensure its sustenance as an integral part of the community activity.

The most challenging areas for environmental conservation in the view of the Project Staff seemed to be severe erosion prone depressions forming gullies and streams near the villages. This area apparently remained unattended. The Government agencies avoided tackling such areas mainly because of it's unproductive nature and the vastness of manpower and the resource required. Since the ownership of most of such areas is vested with the Government, it's status as a no man's land further worsened due to overgrazing.

The earth in such areas are very loose and porous. Such areas are rilled by heavy downpours and torrential rains during the monsoon. This area apparently not being in direct use by the villager seemed neglected for treatment, though understandably it would be the place giving birth to rills and gullies resulting in severe erosion. The adverse effect it would have on the whole ecosystem of the village is beyond any measure.

The Genesis of the Concept

It was in this area the field functionaries wanted to draw the attention of the villagers if the ecosystem of the village had to be restored in a sustained manner. But how could the attention of the villager be best drawn for such a cause?

The ideas and opinions of the field functionaries started pouring in one by one and several discussions were held. Ultimately, majority decided that the best way to attract a villager's attention was to work with her for a day on voluntary basis for reclaiming such areas through 'Shramdan', *i.e.*, voluntary offer of free labour from villager's side. The project staff would be there with the villager to play as a role model for offering "Shramdan" and give various technical guidance on the spot. The staff finally concluded that, perhaps only such endeavour could make the villagers aware and sensitive to this problem which seemed to eat away slowly even the stable terraces. This endeavour would not only sensetise the villagers but also enable them to tackle the problems in the future with their own concerted efforts.

The Translation of the Concept to the Grassroots

A discussion held with the villagers regarding the idea for treating the erosion prone areas interestingly revealed that villagers were more aware and equally concerned about the loss of soil from their village but tackling it was an arduous task, much concern was shown on the helplessness to tackle it at an individual level. So when the proposal to tackle it with collective offer of a day's voluntary labour, *i.e.*, "Shramdan" was placed in front of them, most replied with "Why should not we give a try?"

In the feedback most villagers also expressed that the emphasis on such activity would revitalise and resurge their collective consciousness to tackle their local problems with their own effort and at the same time would revitalise their community feeling. Many older villagers went further to say that such endeavour in fact, if carried in it's proper spirit, would set a very healthy trend in the youngsters of the community and there would be no reason why the community would to find it rewarding to sustain it even in the post-project stage. Some of the older villagers even transpired their sentiments of having done "Shramdan" in a very special way in their village for a number of community development activities especially in the decade just after the independence of the country.

The idea was brilliant and powerful but required courage, dedication, perseverance, a high motivational spirit backed by convincing power in staff to put it into practice.

The approach was extremely challenging for the villagers to tackle the difficult area by transforming the village community to crusaders for environmental conservation. It was getting united to sacrifice a day's labour, stealing time from their busy hours in the paddy field in the monsoon season. The task seemed quite a difficult one, on the face of it and it seemed a challenging task ahead for the field staff to convince, motivate and organise village communities for it.

Thus, keeping in view the challenge ahead, it was decided that all local level technological and socio-cultural initiatives of the villagers and the local resources are to be explored and pulled together in such a manner so that the villagers would find local initiatives interesting, effective and rewarding.

Keeping in mind this very concept, the first round of workshops were organised for field level functionaries and village motivators in the month of February 1997.

The workshop started with a trickle of brainstorming. This was followed by imparting skills on motivation and grassroots strategic planning with local initiatives and use of local resource for the campaign.

After being clear about the basic strategy to be adopted for planning this campaign, the field staff and the field motivators set out into the villages to motivate the villagers and explore how best the campaign could be achieved with their joint effort.

Few villages required mere encouragement to come forward, while with some others, the staff and motivators had to work hard on motivation "Who are we to do it?," "This is next to impossible" were their initial reactions. With the relentless persuasion by the staff, their answer was that of convincing action "We will do it! We will do it and show it to the world."

In this way the seeds of idea for mass campaign were sown in each village, which gradually got nurtured with local ideas and initiatives. When villagers understood it they developed their own strategy to make this campaign a success in each village.

Meanwhile the field staff.tried to study and explore more of the socio-cultural input in each village and encouraged the villagers to use them for this campaign. In this regard the Project Staff wanted to leave no stone unturned, so much so, that they composed one song for the people in local Garhwali language giving a clarion call for joining hands in the campaign.

The meaning of the song goes like this:

Let Us Plant Trees and Save the Village

Oh come! all sisters let us go planting trees,
To fill all our forests with green trees.
Let us plant *Baanj, Burans, Vhimal* and *Kharik,*
and let us ourselves take care of these.

Cutting of trees leads to erosion,
resulting in the flood of the region.
The forest restores nature and water for us,
More of such water means more grains for us.

Friends where ever we see barren land,
Green! Green them with the plant.
Come one, come all let us joint hands in "Shramdan"
To fill our forests and streams with plants.

If soil flows, then water flows with rains,
Then how can we get our sweet grains.
Oh! let us join hands to hold this flow,
Only then our village will prosper and grow.

This song was sang with the villagers in every village meetings and the pamphlets of this song were distributed during the motivation campaign, village meetings and workshops. The message spread like wild fire with each village spontaneously setting their own lyrics to the wording of this song. May be this was their way for making this song more familiar and more absorbing in their native cultural milieu.

Strategic Planning

A. With the Staff

After much exploration work done by the field staff with the local communities on the quantum of different kinds of local support they could wield for this campaign in every village, it was on 23rd of June 1997, the staff decided to sit together to put their findings into strategic planning for translating them into action.

The need was also fell to develop some standard proforma for strategic planning, monitoring and evaluating the contribution of the villagers in the "Shramdan" campaign in each village. The staff worked on it for about three hours through a mutual group discussion and eventually designed two proformas to take into account the quantum of local level individual and collective support that could be garnered by the villagers for the campaign. The proformas, thus, prepared for strategic planning could also be used for monitoring the level of preparation done by the villagers for the campaign. In two hours' discussion which followed, the staff developed proforma to take into account the actual amount of work, that would be performed in each village which involved doing simple exercise with the villagers on the spot right after the planting programme.

B. With the Villagers

After having discussed the operational plan with the staff, 28th June 1997, 29th June 1997 and 30th June 1997 were decided as days to sit with the village representatives from all the villages of the division to finally discuss the action.

These meetings were organised in three different villages taking into consideration the remoteness of the area.

Village Katal—28th June 1997 was attended by 107 villagers from 25 villages and 11 staff members.

Village Bavani—29th June 1997 was attended by 77 villagers from 14 villages, 5 NGO members from 'Janadhar'.

Village Koti-May-Chak—30th June 1997 was attended by 50 villagers from 9 villages and 13 staff members.

On an average 50 per cent of the attendance was by the women representatives. In this way two to five representatives of each village participated in these workshops to discuss with the project staff their plan of action for the campaign and put it down on the papers for record.

The first session of the workshop started with a trickle of brainstorming which triggered exchange of ideas on environmental conservation in the context of local ecosystem and what best could possibly be done at local level using ones own initiative.

In the second session the representative from different villages sat with the local staff to discuss their final strategy and put down the same in the proforma developed by the staff in their workshop of 23rd June 1997 which took into account the following details:

* The date of "Shramdan" in the village.
* The name of the erosion prone area/Nallah/Gully that would be taken up for vegetative treatment.
* A rough map of the erosion prone area/Nallah/Gully spotting it as a location in the village.
* The length and the breadth of the erosion prone area/Nallah/Gully that would be treated.
* The number of cuttings and the saplings of different plant species that would be planted and seed species that would be sown and who would procure it from what source and the distance.
* The number of villagers who would come to participate on that day.
* The name of their task leader chosen for the task of the day.
* Number of different types of implements required for the work and who would bring them.
* The form of traditional ritual villager would like to perform.
* Chief guest on the occasion.
* If villagers wish to call any public representative on the occasion.

After this exercise was done, the representative from each village presented before the gathering their proposed strategic action plans prepared for the day of campaign in their village. In this way villagers were clear about the task they would fulfil with the details of individual as well as collective responsibility for the day. This comprised the second session of the workshop.

In the third session, the village representatives were taken to a nearby eroded area by the Project staff carrying the cuttings and implements like crowbar, *Kutla, Darati* and *Patal* to practically guide them on methods of making good cuttings and methods of sound planting. All these were performed amidst traditional folk songs and drum beatings. Here emphasis was given on:

* Using sharp implements.
* Preparing the cutting in the same day of planting.
* Having a clear identification of the upper and lower portion of cutting.
* Making a deep hole (at least 1 ft.) for planting the cutting.
* Pressing the soil firmly after planting the cuttings.

The delightful demeanour of the participants in this workshop reflected as if the innumerable droplets of ideas and initiatives that had been generated in the villages over the months eventually found a conducive forum to evolve into a continuous stream. As the sessions approached towards its' end it had already taken the shape of a positive storm.

As soon as field exercise on demonstration ended the participants of workshop could not resist the call of their traditional drumbeats which they had been hearing throughout the practical demonstration session. They started tapping their feet and clapping their hands in unison with the rhythm of their folk songs to join in a big group dance wherein staff also joined.

In this way all three days of workshop ended in great jubilation and representatives from every village took oath on the behalf of their village in public that his or her village would burst into action as soon as the cloud bursts for the monsoon.

The Strategy Adopted for Monitoring

The information on strategic planning of each village thus, provided by the village representatives were instantly made into three copies. One set was given to the Chairman of Village Committee (GARIMA) in the form of their action plan, one was given to the local staff for monitoring the action on the spot and one copy was kept in the Divisional Office for collective monitoring purpose. Meanwhile, in the Project Office, specific responsibilities were given to the officers, the field staffs and the motivators for taking part in the campaign with the villagers of each and every village so that no village would be left unattended by the project's representative on the decided day of campaign.

Transformation of the Strategy into Collective Action

The first "Shramdan" campaign commenced in village Banali on 4th July 1997 and then a chain of such campaigns commenced almost daily in one village or the other till 17th August. In this way altogether 44 villages participated 51 times.

The day was celebrated as special day in every village. Villagers first performed *Puja* and offered prayers to their local Deity in a traditional way—some villagers chanted hymns, some blew the counch shells, some rang the bells and beat the drums and some even danced before the Deity to please Her and seek Her blessings for the occasion. It was interesting to note that every Microwatershed have their own local deity residing on the top of the ridge which is revered as most sacred place.

Every village planted their first sapling of sacred trees like *Peepal, Pilkhan* and *Bel* near their temple in the name of God amidst chanting of *Vedic mantras* and tying of sacred thread around the planted sapling as well as in their wrists as per their tradition. Whatever, the villagers had decided were planted in their pre-decided erosion prone area near the village amidst the singing of traditional folk songs and popular drumbeats.

In this way, altogether a total of 86,594 plants were planted of which:

* 62,000 were cuttings of different shrubs and tree species,
* 1,200 Bamboo saplings,
* 13,560 Agave stocks,
* 6,800 tubs of local grass species,
* 3,000 tree plant species,
* 7.250 kg. seeds of Sisam, Khair, Siras and other local species.

Altogether 1,421 villagers were reported to have participated in 44 villages.

The Strategy Adopted for Evaluation

The evaluation of the amount of actual work performed in each village was done through collective self-assessment on the spot right after the planting session. The proformas that were developed by the staff after consulting with the villagers in the workshop held on 23rd June 1997 were used. The proforma was designed in the manner which could be easily understood by the villagers to get it filled and at the same time it left plenty of room for any villager to express views on how one felt about the campaign organised by themselves. The field staff, motivator and village level motivators were trained on how to make the villagers fill this simple evaluation form.

Right after the planting programme, the volunteers of the campaign sat with the local project staff motivators and village level motivators to evaluate their own contribution through a simple exercise and give comments on how they felt about the programme. The evaluation form was geared to collect following set of informations:

* Date of campaign conducted in the village.
* Name of the task leader.
* Number of participants.
* Name of the participants and contribution of each participants in the "Shramdan."
* Total number of species wise cuttings planted, plants planted, grass tubs planted and seeds sown.
* Who was the chief guest.
* Which god/goddess/deity was worshipped before starting the "Sharmdan."
* Comment of group leader.
* Comment of Chairman of Village Committee.
* Comment of public representatives and old people.
* Comment of the village level motivator.
* Comment of village incharge.
* Comment of unit incharge.

The Opinion of the Participants

The participants have given interesting comments on the occasion of their campaign for eco-restoration in their village. Comments from all the participants such as task leaders, villagers, public representatives, village motivators and local project staff are varied and inspiring which have been compiled in the form of a booklet.

These comments vividly reflect the mood of the villagers on the day of the campaign—as a day of both nostalgia and jubilation. Nostalgia, in the sense, the villagers were reminded of old practices of the village when they had done such type of community work and of course, the jubilation, was on the ground that they could feel the revival of that lost practice today.

Thus, summing up the reflections—this day, as perceived by most of the villagers was—a turning point for looking back and thinking ahead.

Selected Remarks

Summing up the experience from this campaign, it was a learning exercise for the project personnel in every stage while working with the people. It clearly reflected that villagers were willing to help themselves for overcoming their overtly perceived threat for the village provided the outside team's message and actions sincerely address such problems.

In this grassroot level exercise, the villagers organised in an unique manner to crusade for the betterment of their otherwise unattended degraded village land by developing an active village forum for self-help. In this exercise, local cultural media was widely explored and used by all the villages to augment their voluntary spirit and mobilise the masses.

Most of the comments from the villagers' end reflect that they felt greatly elated and were impressed by the way they could motivate themselves for doing what they called 'the meaningful work for the village'. It has been expressed in all the villages that they would like to continue this campaign programme from next year onwards in a still better way.

Even the few villages, which, showed relatively low response for gearing enough mass support for this first time exercise, had villagers as evaluators of their own work assisted by the project staff as facilitators. Such a process could construct a shared reality between the project personnel and the villagers about the response of the campaign in these villages. This helped the project staff to sort out the issues that could further be negotiated at the village level to enable the programme to improve it's performance.

The thoughtful comments from all the participants have elated the morale and enthusiasm of the project staff to work with the rural communities for restoring the ecosystem with local efforts and local initiatives into a sustainable practice. The staff could also visualise how such simple exercise could work wonders to bring people of the village together for caring their otherwise neglected common property resource.

In this way such "Shramdan" campaign itself evolved as a very powerful tool to arouse the mass consciousness for restoring environmental degradation by bringing about attitudinal change within the community.

The Watershed Management Projects should come forward to explore more of such local perceived needs, local initiatives and local efforts to build the capacity of the local people and nurture them in a manner so that the villagers find their own efforts with local initiatives more rewarding to handle the problem of environmental degradation. The endeavour as such could flag the issue of concern for the environment as a way of life for a villager in terms of sustainable development of his/her village.

'1998 Shramdan'—The Campaign of the Second Year

Building upon the initial experience in mobilizing mass consciousness on environmental conservation using 'Shramdan' as a tool, the Project went further in the monsoon season of 1998 to scale up this participatory research exercise with the villagers in 59 villages in Rishikesh Division.

The important features of the first year's initiative which influenced the participation of the villagers for the campaign of 1998 were:

* The survival of plants planted in the first year.
* Effectiveness of first year's campaign in ameliorating the overall erosion condition of the treatment spot in each village, *i.e.*, people could see the visible changes as a result of the labour offered by them.

Some challenges for the campaign of 1998 were as follows:

1. How a sustained interest could be geared for adhering to community's offer of labour where the general environment of dependency prevails in a village?
2. How the capacity of local institutions (GAREMAs) could be developed to evolve their own system of managing and promoting this mass campaign.
3. How effective networking of these institutions could be established to augment the mass support?

What Did the Project Gain from the Exercise of 1997?

* This exercise tremendously increased the level of mass consciousness towards environmental conservation especially towards protection of plantation sites. This is evident from the fact that Rishikesh Division could develop nine plantation sties in the year 1998 without fencing.
* After the exercise, the feedback taken from the staff revealed that the protection aspect of plantation started getting discussed more seriously in village meetings.
* This exercise could send a clear message to the people that this Watershed Management Project was primarily meant for protection and promotion of natural resources and environment by people.
* Overall, this exercise was found to be a effective tool to orient the people with the objective and the work ethics of the project.

Strategy to Tackle the Emerging Issues of the Second Year

In the preparatory phase of the second year's campaign there was an extensive experience sharing sessions organised with villagers and the field staff. The suggestions given by the villagers in the first campaign and the valuable experiences shared by the field staff from different villages were shared and analysed for developing a meaningful future strategy.

Name of Unit	*Village*	*Village*	*Village*
Narendranagar	Gwar	Kyarki	Bavani
Thano	Tangoli	Baderna	Dharkot
Bhogpur	Katal	Farti	Suryadhar

When the issue of conducting field evaluation of the above selected villages came up for discussion amongst the Project team in the workshop of 22nd June, the question arose as to 'who would do this evaluation work?'

The project staff was of the view that villagers should be involved for this task. The field staff showed confidence that they would be able to persue the experienced task leaders of the first campaign to take on the task of spot evaluation of these sites to whom the job of conducting the evaluation work and reporting back to the project could be handed over.

Then the question arose 'How to prepare these villagers for this evaluation work?'

Further planning on this issue needed intensive discussion between the staff and the experienced leaders of the first campaign. So this issue was kept as the main agenda item for the ensuing workshop of 23rd June 1998. This was the preliminary workshop to decide the outline of 'Shramdan' exercise of the 2nd year, *i.e.*, 1998 where experienced task leaders of the first year's campaign were invited for planning. Few representatives of new villages were also invited for sharing experience on the development of this participatory exercise.

This meeting was attended by 20 Project personnel, 13 task leaders of the first year's campaign and 10 village representatives of new villages.

The main agenda of the meeting on 23rd June 1998 were:

* The constitution of evaluation team.
* Fixing the criteria for the field evaluation.
* Finalising action plan for evaluation and training arrangements of the evaluation team.

In the workshops of 28th, 29th and 30th June 1998. It was proposed that 3 evaluation teams would be constituted, one for the villages of each functional unit. There would be 5 members in each team, of which, 4 members would be the task leaders of 1st year's exercise and one would be the Chairperson of Gram Resource Management Committee (GAREMA) of new village.

The Chairman of those village committees Gram Resource Management Committee (GAREMAs) whose villages had been selected in the preliminary round of field evaluation for reward were also asked to join the evaluation team but were excluded from the judge's panel.

When the question of fixing the criteria for evaluation came up for discussion, the villagers and the staff together developed following criteria and assigned marks for each criterion as follows:

	Criteria	*Full Mark*
1.	The survival percentage of the total planting stocks planted in 1st year in the village through 'Shramdan'	30
2.	The percentage of population who attended 'Shramdan' against the whole village population	30
3.	The overall assessment on how much the 'Shramdan' input was successful for treating the erosion prone area	40

It was also decided that out of the nine villages selected by the staff and officers in the first round only six villages rated as excellent performance would be visited by the evaluation team of selected villagers for spot verification.

As soon as unit-wise evaluation teams were constituted, it was on 24th June 1998, the members of each team were invited to three field unit offices and were imparted basic training for conducting evaluation work at sight. Each evaluation team was provided with details of 'Shramdan' work done in 1997 in the villages under evaluation. The three evaluation team of each unit conducted their evaluation work based on criteria fixed and brought out their report.

The exercise conducted for evaluating people's contribution in the 'Shramdan' exercise of 1997 was undertaken with due care just before the campaign of 1998. This could bring about a tremendous quality consciousness amongst all the participant villages of the second year's campaign.

Planning at the Grassroots

In the month of June 1998, 28th, 29th and 30th were the dates proposed for meetting with the villagers of different microwatersheds in three different field units. This workshop was to draw the final action plan of each village in line with the key issues identified for the year.

The number of the participants who participated in the workshops were as follows:

Unit	*Village in which Workshop was Organised*	*Date*	*No. of Villages Participated*	*No. of Participants*		
				Woman	*Men*	*Total*
Narendranagar	Gugthyani	28.6.1998	20	57	72	129
Rishikesh	Basantpur	26.6.1998	28	48	99	137
Thano	Koti	30.6.1998	14	37	60	97

The issues that were discussed in these workshops were:

* Quality of the work that would be done, *i.e.*, the planting material, planting site, planting method, planting supervision, etc.
* Protection of planted sites from animals.
* Networking for healthy competition.

* Consolidation of the forums initiated for self-help in each village and searching for means and ways to draw local support.
* Augmenting a strong sense of team spirit in each village.

Some of the practical suggestions and comments given by the villagers in last year's campaign, were read out in the workshop and the participants were requested to comment upon them.

The comments reflected that this campaign had touched villagers' life in many aspects as they went on to say:

1. "We are not getting time for *Shramdan* because the time clashes with our paddy planting time yet this is only the right time to do this job."
2. "We are worried about the protection of the common land where we have given *Shramdan*."
3. "This work gives inspiration to us."
4. "For the first time any government department is considering the value of our culture (Garhwali) in the work."
5. "We feel our community feelings getting rejuvenated and a healthy tradition would set in the village."

Street plays were also organised in these workshops on the theme of conservation of natural resources and maintenance of the common property resources of the village in partnership with a local NGO, *Janadhar*. The theatre was concluded with mass oath taken for devoting at least a day in a year for the treatment of the eroding land of the village in the ensuing monsoon season.

It was made clear to the villagers in the workshops organised on 28th, 29th and 30th June 1998, that if this campaign had to become their movement it had to run on their own support and strength. For that, the role played by the local staff in the campaign of the first year, *i.e.*, (1997) would have to be totally taken over by the villagers in the second year. But it was a real challenge for the staff as to how the quality in 'Shramdan' could be maintained in the process. To make the participants become conscious of it, the best performers of the previous year were awarded in public *a certificate of felicitation and a Durri* for sitting on the ground in their community meetings.

It was reflected upon in the meetings that wherever excellent work had been done in the villages it was because of good leadership, training and supervision. So the strategy developed for supervision in the campaign of second year was as follows:

The villagers who came to offer the 'Shramdan' were divided into groups of 6 villagers each. Of which one was selected as supervisor. He/she would be responsible for motivating others to give quality work. The local project staff would give the technical training to the supervisors any one day before the campaign. It was made optional for the staff to remain in the village on the day of the campaign. It was interesting to note that some of the village representatives drew the attention of other participants so as to perform the initial religious ritual for seeking the blessings of Deity for protecting their work from the natural calamity.

Monitoring and Evaluation

It was decided amongst the staff in a meeting on 22nd June 1998 that monitoring and evaluation work should also be left for the village institution to be accomplished. While looking out for ways and means as to how this could be achieved the staff made elaborate discussion with village representatives on 23rd June. On this issue the participants came out with a concrete and practical suggestion. It proposed that every village would invite a neighbouring villager as a special guest on the day of "Shramdan Abhiyan." He would be the special guest of the village for that day and he would guide and supervise the input of the villagers and report back to the project authorities. And in this meeting the participants named this cadre as "Gramin Parvekshak."

It was very interesting to watch the villagers selecting their "Gramin Parvekshak" from another village in the workshops organised on 28th, 29th and 30th June 1998. Every village representative was requesting the representative of the adjoining villages to be their special guest on the proposed day.

The invited "Gramin Parvekshak" were made to sit separately at the end of the workshops of each day and basic training was given to them for overall supervision and inspection of the work and reporting the work to the Project. The proforma developed for reporting was handed over to them to get them filled on the day of the campaign in the village that they were invited.

Compilation of the Strategic Plan of each Village

The action plan developed by each villages were compiled and tabulated to provide information on the proposed programme of each village. The Chief Project Director, and the Project Director were duly informed about the programme of each village and a request was made to them to attend the "Shramdan" of these villages.

Report Compilation of the Work Done in the Villages in 1998

The formats that were developed by the Project in the "Shramdan Abhiyan" of 1997 for on the spot evaluation of the work were used for 1998 exercise also with minor improvisation. Keeping in view of transforming this exercise into people's movement, the need was felt to elicit more opinion from the people for deeper analysis. This was to explore the existing institutional mechanisms and the support system that could be geared in the future to give the needed impetus to this movement. Need was also felt to identify strong local leaders with leadership quality to take on the issue of preservation of natural resources into a practical movement of the people. For this every village was made to undergo an exercise on guided questionnaires on the day of "Shramdan". Since the Project staff are also important stakeholders of this participatory research exercise, they were also made to undergo an exercise for seeking their opinion and suggestions on this issue.

Transformation of the Strategy into Collective Action

The "Shramdan" campaign of June-August 1998 commenced 61 times in 59 different villages of Rishikesh division where a total of 2317 villagers participated of which 675 were women and 1083 were men.

In this way, altogether a total of 1,05,509 plants were planted in the 2nd year of which:

* 64,108 were cuttings of different shrubs and tree species,
* 16,600 Agave stocks,
* 20,901 tubs of local grass species,
* 3,991 tree plant species,
* 18.5 kg. seeds of Sisam, Khair, Siras and other local species.

In 29 villages, the chief guests were the Panchayat members. In the 'Shramdan' campaign organised by the villagers of village Barkot, District Magistrate of Tehri Garhwal participated in this campaign. This was a source of great encouragement for the community of this village.

The major areas in which the project could scale up this participatory research exercise of the second year were as follows:

1. In the campaign year 1998, the villagers went for the plantation of grass species in larger number which was revealed by the fact that the number of grass tubs planted scooted to 20,901 as against 6,800 grass tubs in the year 1997. This was a major shift towards choosing more people friendly planting material. In this the staff had played instrumental role in explaining and motivating the villagers for planting the grass with good soil binding capacity which would give fodder that would automatically be protected by the villagers living in proximity.
2. One of the innovative strategy adopted in 2nd year's campaign was organising a team of villagers to visit and evaluate last year's treatment sites and rewarding the best performers in public meetings before the commencement of that year's campaign based on such evaluation. The impact of this simple exercise undertaken with due care had tremendous impact on the people to bring consciousness from within on the issues focussed by the project for scaling up the process of organisational learning.

The response of the villagers for two successive years on this campaign had tremendously boosted the morale of the field staff. The aim while working for the next campaign was to be the systems development with the villagers on networking for mass advocacy and sustenance of institutional support for this grassroot campaign. The innovative suggestions were pouring in at the Divisional Office in Rishikesh.

The Third Year's Experience

With the experience gained with the people for two years in organizing the campaign, eventually in 1999 January the mandate of the villagers was sought on how they could organise themselves to take on the responsibility. This would build their capacity to carry forward this process of self-generated innovation in the form of set tradition in their villages.

A massive awareness campaign was led by the project in the monthly meetings of GAREMAs in January 99 followed by facilitation exercise on inter- and intra-village networking on institutionalizing this tradition of tree planting. This led the villagers to form the association of GAREMA as termed by the project staff as "Collection of GAREMAs", *i.e.*, COREMAs. This inter-village association was solely formed based on social affiliation. Altogether 70 GAREMAs formed 14 associations by the end of February 99. The number of GAREMAs varying from 2 to 19 in extreme cases but on an average 4 to 5 villages offered to be under the fold of each COREMA. Two of the villages did not want to come under the fold of any COREMA. The monthly meetings of March 1999 mainly focussed on raising awareness about this nascent federation which was going to take a concrete shape in the months to come to shoulder the responsibility of evaluating the past 'Shramdan' of each village and organising the 'Shramdan campaign' in the 1999 monsoon season. Discussions were held on roles and responsibilities of COREMA and the expectation of the GAREMAs from the COREMA. Meanwhile, the selection of the candidate from each GAREMA for representation in the COREMA was made and much thought was also put in this meetings on the support system that GAREMAs needed to give to the COREMA to enable them to function better to meet the long-term objectives of their campaign. Each GAREMA offered to mobilise a minimum of 2 per cent of their revolving fund for COREMA and agreed to offer at least 10 per cent of their yearly earnings to the COREMA for carrying out the work assigned to the COREMA. Thus by the month of April 1999 all the 14 COREMAs had come into existence with the selection of their working committee members.

Each COREMA started mobilising the villages coming under their fold for the campaign and at the same time started preparing themselves for on-the-spot evaluation of the work done in their respective villages during 1998 "Shramdan" campaign. Meanwhile, the project organized workshops with the COREMA and the GAREMA executive committee members at different microwatersheds. This was to explore the capacity building needs of the COREMA towards evolving a full proof institutional mechanism to sustain this campaign as an established tradition of these villages. In the month of May 1999 COREMA conducted the evaluation of the Shramdan of 1998 of the villages coming under their fold.

In the month of June 1999, this federation organised the public function of the villages coming under their fold and explained how they conducted the performance evaluation of 1998 campaign of the different villages and distributed awards to the best performing villages. The fund for organising the award came from the pooled fund of the GAREMAs into the COREMA. By the end of June 1999, COREMA members were all set to perform the first task given to them by the project, *i.e.*, organising the 'Shramdan' in the tradition of the past two year in each village coming under their fold.

In this way altogether 88 villages came forward and participated in the "Shramdan" campaign of 1999 monsoon season of which in the 18 new villages taken up by the project, the campaign was conducted on the initiative of the project staff and in the rest 68 villages the campaign was totally conducted on the initiative of the COREMA. The 2 old villages which did not want to come under the fold of any COREMA performed "Shramdan" on their own initiative. A total of 66,281 cuttings and plants were planted and 25.1 kg. of seed were sown by the villagers in 86 different erosion prone areas near their villages. Altogether 2,783 villagers had participated of which 1,409 participants were women and 1,274 participants were men.

It was interesting for the project to learn the decrease in the number of the plants planted in the campaign of 1999 despite increase in the number of villages and in the number of villagers from each village who participated in the campaign as compared to the past two years.

While discussing this issue with the Project staff, they opined that villagers now want to go for quality Shramdan to win the award from COREMA in the year 2000. But when the same issue was discussed with the GAREMA and COREMA members it was found that all the villages have somewhat underreported the number of plants planted so that they would be able to show maximum survival percentage to the evaluation team before the monsoon of 2000.

The way with which the COREMA could handle this campaign superbly in the first year has given a lot of answers to the future management of this campaign. The future process development will be to evolve organisational support system to the COREMA from within and outside the village institutions. By showing the role COREMAs could play within the community for social mobilisation and awareness convinced the Project that this nascent federated structure could go a long way for handling important withdrawal responsibilities in relation to each GAREMA coming under their fold. Future process development with the COREMA will mainly focus on the issues pertaining to operationalising the institutional mechanisms in the future "Gram Resource Management Plan" of each village done by the villagers for protection and management of their natural resources regenerated by them. The role of COREMA in the future management of common property resource will be crucial as a guardian of GAREMAs in relation to assessing the performance of each GAREMA, guiding them for qualtiy performance and external networking, taking up policy issues in larger forums and resolving various anticipated inter- and intra-GAREMA conflicts and issues with the other agencies.

The basic objective of this action research is to enable the village communities to innovate and develop simple, low cost and appropriate technology for soil conservation measures which the villagers could easily afford to reduce their vulnerability against the landslide affecting their villages. This initiative has been widely welcomed by the villagers mainly because of the fact that the support partnership which the village institutions normally get from the line agencies for soil conservation measures is grossly inadequate against the quantum of erosion taking place in this fragile area of Shivaliks and the lesser Himalayas. By putting the local knowledge and the initiative to the core of this exercise, the community has been involved in the process of self-generated innovation coupled with institutional capacity building to sustain such innovation. The process being controlled by analysing the results critically by the inter- and intra-village communities has led to vast improvement in the quality of participation. This is in terms of augmenting co-operation for giving due technical attention to the soil conservation problem of the village and adequately sharing the collective responsibility for preserving eco-system. This process of action research over last three years has taught the project staff on how to work with the communities on evolution of systems and the institutions for sustenance of technological innovations at the local level. This in turn has helped to effectively build the capacity of the project staff.

What after 2001?

The Project will end in December 2001. With the process development achieved so far in this participatory research exercise done with the villagers, the project hopes that this campaign would serve as a major instrument to augment the local initiatives to take care of environmental degradation in each micro watershed. This is a much cheaper and effective way after the project withdraws from the villages. The opportunity which the project has is to scale up the process development of this exercise till the year 2001.

2

RURAL WOMEN AND FOOD INSECURITY
What Food Calendars Reveal: A "Longitudinal Study"

AMITAVA MUKHERJEE AND NEELA MUKHERJEE

Introduction

Village Krishna Rakshit Chowk, is in Midnapore District, West Bengal, India. It is in Arjuni Mouza in Kharagpur block I of Midnapore District. The village was visited in 1993. Specifically, the attempt was to study the dynamics of the rural economy through the eyes of villagers. In the process of so doing a Food Calendar prepared by the people (the women) of the village emerged. This provided valuable insights into the different dimensions of food (in) security as portrayed by poor tribal women, who are traditionally responsible for harvesting and gathering food, for processing and intra-household distribution of food, consuming the left overs, often suffering hunger themselves. The village was re-visited in May, 1995 and again in 1998 in an attempt to discern and discuss the changes that may have occurred in the status of the poor households of the village between 1993 and 1995 and between 1995 and 1998. A Second Food Calendar was worked out in 1995 and a third one in 1998. This paper is an analysis of the three Food Calendars.

Conceptual Specification

It would be useful to very briefly outline the concept of food security to be used in this paper. For us food security is ensured where:

(a) there is enough food available in the system.
(b) people have the capacity (purchasing power) to access food;

(c) food that is available is culturally acceptable;
(d) that food accessed and consumed by people have adequate nutrition (quality dimension) and that
(e) there are no institutional barriers to consumption of such food (Mukherjee, 1997(a)).

The above position is derived from Sen's Entitlement and Deprivation Thesis (ED). The entitlement and deprivation thesis, holds that food insecurity can be seen as the characteristics of the person not having enough to eat, which is not tantamount to saying that "there is not enough to eat." It is argued that whether and how food insecurity is related to food availability is a matter for factual investigation. Food insecurity statements are about the relationship of the person to food.

In a private market economy, ownership relations and their mapping with others, play important role in determining food security at the household level amongst others.

The extent to which an individual is food secure depends upon both the person's ownership of food and on the exchange entitlement mapping that he or she faces. Such entitlement mappings include trade based entitlement, production based entitlement and own labour entitlement. (Mukherjee, 1995)

Endowment and Exchange

Clearly, the ED's approach to the food insecurity of an individual concentrates on his or her ability to command food through the legal means available, including the use of production possibilities, trade opportunities, entitlements *vis-a-vis* the state, and other methods of acquiring food. Individuals are food insecure either because they do not have the ability to command enough food, or because the ability to avoid food insecurity is not used. But entitlement failures, direct or indirect, would affect the food security. These failures can be direct entitlement failure and trade entitlement failures. The latter can occur either owing to an autonomous production decline, such as cash crop being destroyed by drought or pest attack, or to an induced decline in output, caused by say insufficiency of demand. Further entitlement failure can occur due to economic changes and unfavourable exchange entitlements.

Let us now turn and see to what extent and why the villagers of Krishna Rakshit Chowk was food insecure over the years.

II. The Methodology and the Process

Traditions, practices, customs and usage have all enjoined upon rural women to assume automatic responsibility for collecting, fuel and fodder, gathering food from forests and commons, fetching drinking water; often traveling long distances, cooking for the household, child rearing, a host of household chores and farm operations. These activities are difficult, time consuming and provide critical support to rural life, but many of them are not directly visible and tangible in economic terms (and indeed not fully accounted for in economic analysis). Hence it is important to understand food security from women's perspective.

Described here are the three food calendars made by rural women, one in 1993, second in 1995 and the third one in 1998, which are analysed in order to highlight three aspects of village life *One,* the knowledge of rural, women in gathering of food from commons, forests and micro-environments, *Two*, their role in such procurement and *Three*, in seasonality of food availability, its shortage and the dependence of the villagers on food from commons, forests and 'micro-environments'. see (Mukherjee and Mukherjee 1994, Mukherjee 1997(b)) for details of the process of making the Food Calendar in 1993.

The Community

The inhabitants of Krishna Rakshit Chat are poor and they belong to the 'Lodha' tribe. The village has 49 households as per the villagers which figure may be at slight variance with the 1991 census figures. Most of the households are landless.

In the three repeated exercises, women were encouraged to prepare food calendars, as a process of participatory rural appraisal. At the beginning, *i.e.*, 1993, women were hesitant and shy: but soon were able to engross into intricate details of food consumption, procurement and also intra household distribution.

Using various locally available material like stones, pebbles, leaves, etc., and traditional knowledge of time and space, women drew on the sand 12 months (as per Hindi calendar) and identified various parameters related to food security.

It is to be noted that across different commodities and months, women have only expressed relative changes in consumption and not absolute quantity of food consumption.

For example, each column in the Food Calendars has to be read as "stand alones", indicating the relative amount of the particular food item (named in the column-head) available in different months. An illustration would clarify the point. Table 2.1, column 1, depicts the pattern of rice consumption. The numbers 15 against Magh and 9 against Phalgun show that, consumption of Rice in Magh was higher than in Phalgun. Similarly, the number 2 against Poush indicates that consumption of rice was even lower in Poush than in Phalgun and so on. These numbers do not, indicate the absolute quantum of rice consumed, such as 15 kgs. or 9 kgs., etc.. Additionally, numbers across the columns such as in column 1 and column 2, are non-comparable and non-relative. That is the number 15 under rice against Magh in column 1 when compared with number 13 under potatoes against Magh also, does not indicate that consumption of rice is higher in Magh than the consumption of potatoes.

The same holds good for all the columns of all the tables.

III. The 1993 Food Calendar

The 1993 Food Calendar (which was prepared in Magh, corresponding to mid-January to mid-February) is given in Table 2.1.

The Two Food Systems

There are two food systems which can be identified from the food calendar. The food *produced* on agricultural land by application of technology (in the economic sense) which may be called food from the "Primary Food System." Examples of such food are rice and potatoes. *Two,* food collected, gathered and hunted from common property resources, forests and "micro-environments" (Chambers, 1990) which may be called food from the "Secondary Food System." Wild fruits, herbs, plants, honey, gums, leaves, tubers, birds, small animals, fish, snails, etc., are typical examples of food generated by the secondary food system. (Mukherjee, A., 1994).

The Seasonal Variations

The 1993 Food Calendar as shown in Table 2.1 has some more important features in terms of food availability.

As mentioned earlier, first, the basket of food consumed can be divided into two groups principal food items (rice, potatoes and pulses) and secondary food items (leaves, fish, fruits from commons, forests and micro-environments and wild animals).

Second, rice consumption reaches a peak in "Magh" (mid-January to mid-February) after which it declines until "Chaitra" (mid-March to

TABLE 2.1: Seasonal Food Calendar 1993

Month	*Rice*	*Potato*	*Pulses*	*Vegetables***	*Fruits**	*Food from Water Sources***	*Other from Wild*	
	(1)	(2)	(3)	(4)	(5)	(6)	(7)	(8)
Magh (mid-January to mid-February)	15	13	3	Cabbage			Wild borums, wild rabbits	
Phalgun (mid-February to mid-March)	9	11	2	Spinach			'Neem' leaves	
Chaitra (mid-March to mid-April)	4	4	2	Pumpkin		Fish and wild water plants		
Baisakh (mid-April to mid May)	4	3	1	'PUI' leaves (herbs)	Mango* Jackfruit*	Fish, snails and wild water plant		
Jyaistha (mid-May to mid-June)	4	4	2	'Lota' leaves (herbs)	Mango* Jackfruit*	Fish, wild water plant		
Ashar (mid-June to mid-July)	4	3	3	'Jhinge' (near to Sukinni)				
Srabon (mid-July to mid-August)	4	4	5	Papaya				
Bhadra (mid-August to mid-September)	4	3	3	Greem banana		Fish & Snails		
Aswin (mid-September to mid-October)	4	3	2					
Kartick (mid-October to mid-November)	2	3	2	Raddish leaves				
Agrhayan (mid-November to mid-December)	2	4	5	Tomato				
Poush (mid-December to mid-January)	2	9	6	Brinjal			Wild rabbits	

Source: Prepared on February 4, 1993, by Women Group, village Krishna Rakshit Chak, West Bengal.

Notes: The numbers specified under rice, potato and pulses represent the number of stones used by the village to show the availability of the relative item of food.

* Fruits from some trees growing near ponds and elsewhere in the village.

** From CPR and forest.

Village Analysts: Namita Mallik, Binapani Dandapat, Pratima Bhakta, Sushila Malik.

Facilitator: Neela Mukherjee.

mid-April), to remain stationary until mid-September to mid-October), following which it further declines by almost half of the earlier period.

Third, eating of potatoes follow approximately the same trend as rice for the months of Magh (mid-January to mid-February) and Phalgun (mid-February to mid-March) and then declines sharply and stays at a lower level during the period from Chaitra (mid-March to mid-April) to Agrahyan (mid-November to mid-December) and picks up again in Poush (mid-December to mid-January).

Fourth, intake of pulses as an element of food in the diet of the villagers touches an "all time" low in the month of Baisakh (mid-April to mid-May) and is higher in the months of Srabon (mid-July to mid-August). Agrahyan (mid-November to mid-December) and Poush (mid-December to mid-January), as shown in the 1993 Food Calendar.

Finally, the villagers consume a variety of food gathered from different sources in the secondary food system, depending upon their availability.

In terms of food security arguments, there occurs a fall in availability of food in certain months and there could also be seen as decline in the nutritional value of food consumed during the same months. Thus, there is inter-month variation in the intensity of food insecurity from both food availability and food quality perspectives.

The women's group pointed out in course of a semi-structured interview, held during the preparation of the food calendar, that with depletion of common property resources, forests and degradation of ponds, the support received from these sources during 'hunger periods' as sources of food has declined considerably over time.

The food generated by the secondary food systems accountable to compensate the decline in 'quality' of food consumption especially through primary food system.

It needs to be underscored that during two distinct periods in the year, namely, that during Chaitra, Baisakh and Jyaistha (mid-March to mid-June), and again during Bhadra, the availability of fish increases very significantly. Because it constitutes the peak summer period and the home of fish (namely, ponds, rivulets and other water bodies) dry up and the catch becomes easier and hence the availability of fishes increase. And concurrently, it is also the lean period leaving the villagers with enough slack time to venture into fishing and collecting snails and water weeds. As the rains set in, with the onset of the south-west monsoon, in Ashar (mid-June to mid-July), the water bodies swell, fishing becomes more arduous. Villagers, also find employment with the start of the cultivation season, and have little time, to engage in gathering and hunting. Again such fish gathering activity takes place during Bhadra (mid-August to mid-September), after nearly two months of rain (in Ashar and Srabon, that is, mid June to mid-August), the rivulets, ponds and other water bodies start overflowing flooding nearby fields and meadows. (The rainfall pattern is that the month of Bhadra, unlike Ashar and Srabon (mid-June to mid-August, witness sharp showers only on certain days). With such flooding come fishes and snails flow into the fields. The water recedes after the rains stop (or sometime thereafter), leaving in the mud and in small puddles strewn all over the fields and in meadows, fishes and snails which the, villagers catch/collect. Bhadra is also a month of low-key agricultural activity, leaving the poor people with spare time to indulge in gathering activities. Thus, the supply of fish for consumption as secondary food increases considerably.

The Two Hunger Periods

Columns 2, 3 and 4 of the Table 2.1 reveal two clear 'hunger periods', for the village Krishna Rakshit Chak. The first 'hunger period' occur in the proverbial summer months of Bengal, namely, in Chaitra, Baisakh and Jyaistha (mid-March to mid-June) taken together, when availability and consumption of rice and potatoes come down to their lowest level and the availability and level of pulses consumed are rock-bottom. These coupled with acute paucity of employment in the rural sector, during this period, leads to entitlement failure. Table 2.6 give the employment calendar for the year. The second 'hunger period' occurs during the months of Aswin and Kartick (mid-September to mid-November) where again a fall in availability of rice and pulses, and hence by a decline in their consumption increases hunger.

During the first 'hunger period' the bounties of common property resources and forests come to the rescue of the poor villagers (see columns 5, 6 and 7 of the Table 2.1). Fish, snails and water-weed plants collected from the water bodies compensate, at least partially, the loss in protein intake caused by a fall in consumption of pulses. The reduction in calorie intake caused by declining consumption of rice and potato is partially offset by the availability of fruits, like mangoes and jackfruits from village commons.

During the second 'hunger period', the consumption of pulses falls (reaching 2 in Aswin) and then rises in Kartick but then the consumption of rice reaches the second low plateau, (dropping down to 2 from 4 in Aswin). This is also the period when employment opportunities in the rural sector are limited as the harvesting season is yet to get underway and other economic activities are not enough to provide income to the poor to buy food from the market as well. Unlike the first hunger period, the second 'hunger period' has no safety net from the CPR and micro-environment to help the rural poor to tide over their 'increased hunger'. Significantly enough this is the time when vegetables and leaves from the CPR also reach the lowest level. And this, incidentally, is the period which 'roughly corresponds with the major festivities of the area, namely, Durga Puja, Bhatri Dwitiya and Kali Puja (Depawali), which contribute towards increasing the distress of the poor, involving huge social expenditures.

IV. The 1995 Food Calendar

After about two years, in 1995 we returned to Krishna Rakshit Chak to meet the villagers. Nothing much has changed the terrain, the landscape, the topography, the people, their poverty, the huts and even the vagaries of nature. The warmth, the forthrightness and the enthusiasm of the villagers remained undiminished. The women were as enthusiastic as they were in 1993 to work out the food calendar a second time over. There was only one difference: the rural women already had the "technology" to develop the food calendar. There was scant need to facilitate the production. The women produced a food calendar with the same ease with which they proverbially cook food for their households, everyday, 365 days a year.

Once the 1995 Food Calendar was ready, a discussion was held with the villagers with open ended questions to understand the dynamics underlying the two Food Calendars. The 1995 Food Calendar is in Table 2.2. Since the 1995 Food Calendar was prepared towards the end of the Bengali Month of "Chaitra" (which roughly corresponds to mid-March to mid-April), the 1995 Food Calendar starts in "Chaitra." In order to make the 1995 Food Calendar comparable to the 1993 Food Calendar, we re-arranged only the months so that the 1995 Food Calendar can be read as starting (as in case of the 1993 Food Calendar) in Magh (corresponding to mid-January to mid-February). The re-arranged 1995 Food Calendar is given in Table 2.3.

The 1995 Food Calendar indicates like the 1993 Food Calendar, that the poor people are dependent upon both the primary and secondary food system. The 1995 Food Calendar exhibits very substantial variations in inter-month consumption of food, which reaches its lowest during the months spanned by Chaitra to Kartick (both months included) that is, from mid-March to mid-November. This implies that people have enough food for approximately 4 months in a year. The dominance of rice and potatoes in the consumption basket of the poor reflects the food preference of the people in that part of India. However, consumption of potatoes vanished during Bhadra, Aswin and Kartik (mid-August to mid-November). Columns 4 to 9 Table 2.3, shows that a large part of the diet of the poor households are made up of only Rice and Potatoes. The consumption of fish and snails is significant only during the months following the monsoons. Consumption of potato vanished, according to the villagers, during certain months of 1995, because the overall rise in prices, did not allow them the luxury of consuming potatoes between Bhadra and Kartick (mid-September to mid-November).

TABLE 2.2: Food Calendar 1995 (Scored out of 10 Stones)

Month	*Rice*	*Potato*	*Pulses*	*Vegeth.****	*Fruits**	*Fish****	*Snails****
(1)	(2)	(3)	(4)	(5)	(6)	(7)	(8)
Chaitra (mid-March to mid-April)	5	3	—	—	—	—	—
Baisakh** (mid-April to mid-May)	4	3	—	—	—	—	—
Jyaistha (mid-May to mid-June)	4	3	—	—	—	—	—
Ashar (mid-June to mid-July)	4	2	—	—	—	—	—
Srabon (mid-July to mid-August)	6	3	—	—	—	—	—
Bhadra (mid-August to mid-Sept.)	2	—	—	—	—	10	—
Aswin (mid-Sept. to mid-Oct.)	2	—	—	—	—	10	5
Kartick (mid-Oct. to mid-Dec.)	3	—	—	—	—	10	6
Agrahayan (mid-Nov. to mid-Dec.)	10	4	—	—	—	—	—
Poush (mid-Dec. to mid-January)	10	4	—	—	—	—	—
Magh (mid-Jan. to mid-Feb.)	8	4	—	—	—	5	—
Phalgun (mid-Feb. to mid-Mar.)	7	3	—	—	—	6	—

Notes: The numbers specified under rice and potato represent the number of stones.
* Fruits from some trees growing near ponds and elsewhere in the village.
** This is the first month of the Bengali Calendar.
*** From CPR and forest.

Village Analysts and facilitator: Same as Table 2.1.

The variations in the levels of food consumed from month to month shows a pattern: when more food is locally available (harvesting season) the consumption level goes up, when food availability goes down locally (cultivating season and the pre-harvesting season), level of food consumption also falls. It is important to recognize that variations in the levels of food consumption of the poor, are caused both by "price effect" and "quantity effect." The "price effect" and the "quantity effect" are more important (in 1995 than in 1993) because the role of food from the Secondary Food System in providing food for the poor had assumed lesser importance in 1995 than earlier observed. The picture is reversed at least partially in 1998.

TABLE 2.3: Food Calendar 1995 (Scored out of 10 stones)

Month	*Rice*	*Potato*	*Pulses*	*Vegeth.***	*Fruits**	*Fish***	*Shails***	*Others from Wild*
(1)	(2)	(3)	(4)	(5)	(6)	(7)	(8)	(9)
Magh (mid-Jan. to mid-February)	8	4	—	—	—	—	—	—
Phalgun (mid-Feb. to mid-March)	7	3	—	—	—	—	—	—
Chaitra (mid-March to mid-April)	5	3	—	—	—	—	—	—
Baisakh (mid-April to mid-May)	4	3	—	—	—	—	—	—
Jyaistha (mid-May) to mid-June)	4	3	—	—	—	—	—	—
Ashar (mid-June to mid-July)	4	2	—	—	—	—	—	—
Srabon (mid-July to mid-August)	6	3	—	—	—	—	—	—
Bhadra (mid-August to mid-Sept.)	2	—	—	—	—	10	—	—
Aswin (mid-Sept. to mid-Oct.)	2	—	—	—	—	10	5	—
Kartick (mid-Oct. to mid-Nov.)	3	—	—	—	—	10	6	—
Agrhayan (mid-Nov. to mid-Dec.)	10	4	—	—	—	—	—	—
Poush (mid-Dec. to mid-January)	10	4	—	—	—	—	—	—

Source: Prepared by Women Group, May 1995, Village Krishna Rakshit Chak, West Bengal.

Notes: The numbers specified under rice, potato and pulses represent the number of stones used by the village women to show availability of the relative item of food.

* Fruits from some trees growing near ponds and elsewhere in the village.

** From CPR and forest.

V. The 1998 Food Calendar

We returned to Krishna Rakshit Chak again in 1998 and had a repeat of preparing a Food Calendar. The Food Calendar is in Table 2.4.

TABLE 2.4: Seasonal Food Calendar 1998: Village Krishna Pakshit Chak

Months	*Rice*	*Potatoes*	*Pulses*	*Vegetable from CPR***	*Fruits***	*Fish* from CPR*	*Snails** etc.*	*Others** from wild*
(1)	(2)	(3)	(4)	(5)	(6)	(7)	(8)	(9)
Baisakh	3	3		Brinjal				
Jaistha	3	3	✓	Kalmi Sak, Susmi Sak, Gim sak			Snails, Jal geri	Jhingae
Ashar	3	1		Wild Potatoes Mushrooms		Fish		
Srabon	4	1				Weeds	✓	
Bhadra	3					Laatha, Chang, Fusati Magur	Snails	
Ashwin	3			Jhingae Borbotee Snake Gourd		Punti Mogur Chang		
Kartick	3			Sak, Seem, Pui sak		Fish		
Aghrayan	12	2				Fish		
Poush	12	2		Sak Raddish				
Magh	10	6				Some fish		
Phalgun	8	4		✓		Samuk, Fish, Jhinuk		
Chaitra	5	4					✓	Rabbits

Notes: ✓ Denotes occasionally. Insignificant amounts. Not worth mentioning.
* Mogur, Laatha, Chang.
** From CPRs, forests and micro-environments.

The 1998 Food Calendar reveals a food security picture which is pretty much consistent with the portrayals of the 1993 and 1995 Food Calendars. In Aghrayan (mid-November to mid-December). Poush (mid-December to mid-January) and Magh (mid-January to mid-February), the food intake of the poor villagers is the highest, rice and potatoes being the major items of food consumed. That is, immediately after the harvest, people are generally well fed. During Phalgun (mid-February to mid-March) and Chaitra (mid-March to mid-April), the consumption of rice and potatoes fall, but they still have substantial (relatively speaking) food to eat. By the time the proverbial Bengal Summer sets in, in Baisakh (mid-April to mid-May), food consumption falls to low level

TABLE 2.5: Seasonal Food Calendar 1998 (Rearranged): Village Krishna Pakshit Chak

Months	*Rice*	*Potatoes*	*Pulses*	*Vegetable** from CPR*	*Fruits**	*Fish* from CPR*	*Snails***	*Others** from wild*
(1)	(2)	(3)	(4)	(5)	(6)	(7)	(8)	(9)
Magh	10	6				Some fish		
Phalgun	8	4		✓		✓		
Chaitra	5	4						Rabbits
Baisakh	3	3		Kalmisak, Susmi Sak, Gim Sak		Boal, Tangra Punti Kucho Chingri	Jal Geri Shamuk (Snails)	
Jaistha	3	3		Susmi Sak, Gima Sak, Kalmi			Jal Geri, Shamuk (Snails)	
Ashar	3	1		Wild Potatoes Mushroom		✓		
Srabon	4	1				Weeds		
Bhadra	3					Laatha, Chang, Magur Crabs Punti	Snails	
Ashwin	3			Jhingaee, Borbotee, Snake gourd		Punti Magur Chang, Laatha		
Kartick	3			Seem, Pui Sak		Fish		
Aghrayan	12	2				Fish		
Poush	12	2		Sak				

Notes: ✓ Denotes occasionally. Insignificant amounts; not worth mentioning.
* Magur, Laatha, Chang.
** From CPR and Forest.

(particularly so for rice) and continues to be so till Kartick (mid-October to mid-November), for seven months. the situation assumes extreme severity in the three months of Bhadra (mid-August to mid-September), Aswin (mid-September to mid-October) and Kartick (mid-October to mid-November), when the only staple food that the village consume is rice, the consumption of potatoes vanishes and there are no pulses.

TABLE 2.6: Employment and Wages in Krishna Pakshit Chak (1998)

Months	*Wages*	*Days of Employment (W)*	*Days of Employment (M)*
Magh	Rs. 30 + Puffed Rice	10-15 days Winnowing	5-10 days Earth work
Phalgun	Rs. 30-40 per sq. ft.	5-10 days Carrying	2-5 days Digging for Stones
Chaitra	—	Some work Boro Paddy Harvesting	Some work Selling of Eucalyptus
Baisakh	—	—	5-6 days
Jaistha	—	—	1-2 days in HH of Landlords
Ashar	Rs. 30 + Puffed Rice	—	1-2 Preparing field of LL
Srabon	Rs. 30 + Puffed Rice	15-16 days Transportation	15-16 days Cultivation work
Bhadra	—	—	—
Ashwin	Rs. 30	4-5 days Weeding	—
Kartick	Rs. 25 + one meal (W) Rs. 30 + one meal (M)	10 days Harvesting	10 days Carrying, storing, etc. 15-20 days
Aghrayan	Rs. 30 + puffed Rice (W) Rs. 50 + puffed. Rice (M)	15-20 days	15-20 days
Poush	Rs. 30 + puffed Rice	—	15 days Husking

Note: 'M' stands for Men and 'W' for Women.

Thus, there is a long hunger period from Baisakh (mid-April to mid-May) through Kartick (mid-October to mid-November). There is a less severe hunger period in the months of Phalgum (mid-February to mid-March) and Chaitra (mid-March to mid-April). There are then three clear phases:

(a) Aghrayan to Magh, people have enough to eat.
(b) In Phalgun and Chaitra, hunger sets in.

(c) For seven months, thereafter from Baisakh (mid-April to mid-May) to Kartick (mid-October to mid-November), the village face severe hunger.

During the severe hunger period, the people are saved of an even greater hunger by the food that they gathered and collected from Common Property Resources. That is, when food generated from the primary food system declined and declined substantially, food from the secondary food system came to the rescue of the hungry. A whole variety of Sak (leafy vegetables), fish, snails and small animals added variety, vitamins and palate to the food of the villagers.

The 1998 Food Calendar generally follows the same pattern as the 1995 Food Calendar and the inter-month variation in food consumption seems to be a function of availability of food in the system. However, the importance of food from the secondary food system in eliminating hunger (or severity of hunger) which had dwindled in 1995 *vis-a-vis* 1993, had returned. And this, remarkably enough, is because a large tank (called Rajbandh), which used to be auctioned by the Panchayat, is under dispute and hence could not be auctioned. Right to the produce of the rank remains disputed. As a result the villagers access the produce of the tank, which explain the return of the food from the secondary food system in reducing hunger in Krishna Rakshit Chak in 1998.

VI. The Similarities in the Three Food Calendars

There are certain important similarities in the 1993 Food Calendar, the 1995 Food Calendar and the 1998 Food Calendars. *First,* is the persistence of long hunger periods depicted by all the Food Calendars though there are differences in their intensity and duration, to which we will return later. This implies that despite there being apparently no "systemic" shortage of food, reflected by "record" harvest from the primary food system, and a burgeoning buffer food stock with the Government, hunger was a common feature in 1993 and was still as much, if not more, a characteristic of the village life in 1995 and 1998 as well. The *second,* similarity brought out by the three Food calendars, is the dominance of starch in the diet of the people, in terms of rice and potato intake. This is reflective of a cultural trait of that part of India, where rice and potatoes are inseparable components in the diet of the people. The *third,* the three Food Calendars indicate that for the poor households of the village the major source of protein nutrition remains the food collected from common property resources, particularly water sources, and forests and micro-environments. More importantly, the relative dependence on food from the secondary food system, particularly for protein in 1998 and 1995 *vis-a-vis* 1993 has increased in good measure though whether the absolute amounts of protein intake from this source have actually increased or declined in either 1995 or 1998 from the earlier level could not be determined.

VII. And the Dissimilarities

If there are similarities in the three Food Calendars, there are dissimilarities as well. And the dissimilarities in the Food Calendars are telling and require serious consideration. *First,* pulses which were important components of the food basket shown by the 1993 Food calendar, have vanished from the diet of the poor from 1995. Pulses provide essential proteins and nutrients to the poor households in our rural economy. Absence of pulses from the diet of the poor indicates that the quality of food in terms of proteins has deteriorated in 1995 *vis-a-vis* 1993. *Second,* the intake of *vegetables* and *fruits* which were significant in 1993 Food Calendar, vanished in 1995. This implied that the quality of food in 1995 in terms of essential vitamins and fibre intake had also deteriorated though there was a partial recovering in 1998, on this account. *Third,* the consumption of other kinds of food, herbs and leaves, from common property resources, forests and "micro-environments," were gone in 1995 and was limited to consumption of fishes and snails over two and three months respectively. This means that elements of the consumption basket shown in the 1993 Food Calendar which added nutrition, palate and variety to the food basket of the poor households, were gone in 1995. Because of the dispute over Rajbandh (the tank) some amount of variety and palate was added to the diet, but one can not definitively say, if it was restored to the 1993 level. *Fourth,* and the most important dissimilarity, is that instead of two shorter hunger periods in 1993, (from Chaitra to Jyaistha corresponding to mid-March to mid-June and from Aswin to Kartick corresponding to mid-september to mid-November) with some relief in between, the 1995 Food Calendar shows that now there was one long hunger period from Chaitra to Kartik (both months inclusive), spanning eight months and increasing in intensity all the more during the latter part of the hunger period, *viz.,* during Bhadra, Aswin and Kartick. The longer hunger period of 1995, more or less, persists in 1998 as well.

The implication, of the differences in the two Food Calendars of 1993 and 1995 and 1998 are serious. It is apparent that in 1995 and in

1998 the total food consumption *per se* of the poor households of Krishna Rakshit Chak had gone down, from an already low level. Concurrently the "quality" of food in terms of fibre and vitamins content had also deteriorated in 1995. Thus, relative hunger had increased in 1995 *vis-a-vis* 1993. Additionally the Food Calendar in 1995 (as opposed to 1993 revealed a consumption pattern that was less palatable and certainly less varied. The dissimilarities in the Food Calendars of 1993 on the one hand and 1995 and 1998 Food Calendars on the other, indicate that on the whole, the poorer people faced greater food insecurity in 1995 than they faced in, 993; they had lower quantity of food available, they accessed lower amounts of food and finally they accessed food that was less in nutritional value.

If we now compare the 1993, 1995 and the 1998 Food calendars, the picture remains the same hunger has increased since 1993, but in 1998 due to greater availability of food from the secondary food system, the severity of hunger was less than in 1995. The "elongated hunger period" of 1995 (as compared to two hunger periods of 1993) persists even in 1998.

VIII. The Probe

In keeping with the accepted methods of "interviewing" the Food calendars, a discussion with the villagers mostly women ensured on what the 1995 and 1998 Food Calendars revealed. There were two components of the discussion: *One* on what was available in 1995 and 1998, and *two*, on what was not available in 1995 but was available in 1993 and what was available in 1995 but not available in 1998. First things first.

Between 1993, 1995 and 1998 there was no significant change in the dietary habits of the people, insofar as they continue to prefer and consume rice as the principal staple food. The intake of rice, as seen from Column 2 of the Table 2.3, roughly corresponds to an U-Shaped curve with almost a flat bottom. It is relatively high in Magh (mid-January to mid-February) and falls steadily to a lowest point in Ashwin (mid-September to mid-October) and then again rises dramatically in the two months of Aghrayan and Poush (mid-November and mid-January). Clearly, the consumption of rice is higher immediately after the harvest (Aghrayan and Poush corresponding to mid-November to mid-January) and then falls steadily through the summer, to reach the lowest point during the cultivation season immediately proceeding the harvesting of the next crop. That is, the consumption of rice apparently varies in direct proportion to its availability in the village, its availability is highest after harvesting in a season and lowest before the harvest in the following season.

We have mentioned earlier that most of the villagers of Krishna Rakshit Chak are landless labourers belonging to Lodha tribe. Basically, they are not producers of rice and potatoes, and they purchase these goods from the market for consumption by selling their labour. They, therefore, explained that the level of rice consumption was determined both by rice availability (the supply factor) which regulated the price of rice in the market, and availability of employment (power to access the available food), though the former was the dominant factor determining food consumption level.

During Aghrayan (mid-November to mid-December), employment opportunities are available in the fields and farms, for harvesting paddy, both in the village and in adjoining villages. The average wage hovers around Rs. 30 per day together with a breakfast of "puffed rice," and fortunately both men and women find work. During Poush (mid-November to mid-January), while men find work in threshing and winnowing paddy, the women find work in husking rice.

Finding work is more difficult in Poush than in Aghrayan, but the availability of rice is higher in Poush (mid-November and mid-January) and hence the price of rice is relatively low. The villagers, therefore, not only consume more rice during these two months but are also able to buy rice to store food, for consumption during the next two months Magh and Phalgun, (corresponding to the period mid-January to mid-March).

During Magh to Phalgun, (mid-January to mid-March) the on-farm activities dry up and the villagers, therefore, make a living by selling fish and firewood, they collect from the water bodies and forests respectively and are able to maintain a certain level of consumption, both from these off-farm earnings and by using foodgrains (rice mainly) stored during the previous period of Aghrayan-Poush (mid-November to mid-January). From Chaitra (mid-March) onwards life becomes difficult as not only employment opportunities and off-farm incomes dwindle, the availability of primary food (rice and potatoes) in the local market goes down, reflecting in a rise in their prices. As a result the villagers cut into their consumption level of rice, successively reducing the intake of potatoes until it becomes zero in Bhadra, Aswin and Kartik (mid-August to mid-November).

IX. Food Insecurity in Terms of Employment Deprivation Thesis (ED)

In terms of the ED thesis, there could be food insecurity in the households of the village either due to direct entitlement failure or exchange or trade entitlement failure.

If we examine the primary food system during 1993; the villagers being landless there could not have been any direct entitlement failure because they did not produce their own food. Their food security or insecurity was not dependent on security or insecurity arising out of endowment failure but entitlement mapping that they faced. Trade entitlement failure faced by the villagers during the months of Chaitra, Baisakh and Jaistha (mid-March to mid-June) and during Aswin and Kartick (mid-September to mid-November) in 1993, was due to reduction in employment opportunities and a rise in prices, because of relative scarcity of food in the system. During the remaining seven months of the year, food security was ensured through trade entitlement, made possible by higher employment and/or higher availability of food due to harvests.

In 1995, like in 1993, the food insecurity in term of the primary food system, of the villagers was due to exchange entitlement failure, caused by fall in employment and rise in prices of foodgrains during the hunger period. The tow hunger periods of 1993, got elongated to one long hunger period from Chaitra to Kartick (mid-March to mid-November) because of the general rise in prices that had forced the villagers to forego consumption of potatoes and reduce the consumption of rice in the months of Bhadra, Aswin and Kartick (mid-August to mid-November).

If we look at the *Secondary Food System,* depicted by the 1993 Food Calendar, poor households had direct entitlement of food from the secondary food system. They could reduce hunger because their direct entitlement from common property resources, micro-environment and forests was not jeopardised. In 1995, there was direct entitlement failure in the secondary food system caused by a reduction in output of secondary food from these sources and denial of access to such food by others who owned some of these *sources* which was akin to alienation of land from a landowner, who uses land for production of food.

Significantly, direct entitlement of the poor of secondary food was reduced due to the emergence of a market for secondary food—those who downed some of these sources sold food produced from the micro-environments in the open market to meet their needs. Therefore, in case of the Secondary Food System, the 1995 Food Calendar indicates that direct entitlement failure can occur, where market for such goods emerge. But the access has increased in 1998, due to the fact that privatization efforts were not successful.

We can interpret the collection, gathering and hunting of food from the secondary food system, as being exchange based, that is, the people exchanged their labour for the vegetables, fruits, fish, snails, etc., produced by the Secondary Food System. In that event, there was exchange entitlement failure as the rate of exchange of secondary food *vis-a-vis* labour, moved adversely against the villagers of Krishna Rakshit Chak, at least clearly for 1995.

If we look at the 1998 Food Calendar, the situation of food insecurity from the Primary Food System, was caused by a failure of exchange entitlement. The pattern was similar to what was seen in 1993 and 1995. However, the direct entitlement failure from the Secondary Food System causing food insecurity was eliminated (at least partially) in 1998, as the villagers could exchange their labour for food gathered and collected from the Rajbandh (the tank) whose usufruct could not be auctioned and hence became accessible to the villagers for their use. The dispute regarding ownership of the produce of Rajbandh (the tank) turned out to be the saviour of the poor people.

X. Role of CPR and Hunger Periods

We have mentioned earlier that, whereas, there were two hunger periods in 1993, the *first* hunger period in the 1995 Food Calendar runs for almost eight months at a stretch. We also indicated that the peak segment of the hunger period of Bhadra, Aswin and Kartik, (mid-August to mid-September) as also the segment from Chaitra to Shrabon, in 1995 is more severe than the *two* hunger periods in 1993 (one from Chaitra to Jaistha (mid-March to mid-May) and the second, from Aswin to Kartik (mid-September to mid-November). If we look at columns (2), (3) and (4), of Table 2.1, and compare with columns (2), (3) and (4) of Table 2.3, it will be apparent, that as against 5 months of hunger with a short period of respite in between, in 1993, the 1995 Food Calendar reveals eight months of persistent hunger. Similarly, Table 2.6, indicates one long hunger period with varying intensity of hunger. The length of the hunger period has increased by three months, or by about 60 per cent between 1993 and 1995, and continued to be so in 1998.

It is also seen from columns (5) to (8) of Table 2.1, against the same column numbers of Tables 2.3 and 2.5, that whereas in the hunger periods of 1993 common property resources and micro-environment provided "hunger food" to the poor to reduce both their absolute hunger and relative hunger, in 1995 the availability of food is too little from the secondary food system, during the extended hunger period depicted by the 1995 Food Calendar. Therefore, not only has the hunger period been extended but also the intensity of the hunger over the period has increased. In fine, then the poor households suffered hunger in 1995 and in 1998 over longer periods than in 1993 and, at once, they are relatively more hungry as well. This was a sad revelation that the cabbage, pumpkin, spinach, Pui saag, leaves, herbs, green banana, mango, jackfruit, wild water plants, etc., which found mention in the 1993 Food Calendar, were all gone in 1995 and 1998. During or around 1993, the poor households had free access to sizable amounts of those "hunger foods" from fields of relatively well-off farmers (who did not consume them), but during 1995 and thereafter, due to their (the relatively well off farmers') inability to make both ends meet in the face of rising prices they have started selling these "hunger foods," produced in their fields in the local market to supplement their income. The average level of ongoing prices of some of these hunger foods in the nearby markets of Charkabani, Khemasuli, Tangra, Golbazar and Kalai Kunda Gate No. 2, were Bitter Gourd-3 pieces for Re. 1; Susmi Sak—Re. 1 for 3 bundles; Kalmi sak—Rs. 2 a kg., Thankuni Sak—Rs. 3.50 a kg. and Snails & Fish—at varying prices.

However, in 1998, the market situation remained the same, but the Panchayat could not auction the tank and hence the villagers had access to its produce and due to the dispute over Rajbandh, the tank, the supply of food from the Secondary Food System had increased. Hence, food provided by the CPRs and micro-environment was again available (even after their sale) for consumption to deal with hunger now, as they were available in 1993. In one sense, they have become less hungry in 1998 but suffered longer periods of hunger in 1998 as against five years ago than before.

The villagers pointed out though, that in 1995 and 1998 *vis-a-vis* 1993, the total "output" of "hunger foods," *per se*, had fallen, as the area under common lands (on which a portion of hunger foods grew) is shrinking. Common lands are being diverted to other uses such as social forestry for timber. While no accurate figure for this diversion could be obtained, the poor households did emphasise that it has been significant according to their reckoning in recent years.

XI. Impact on Women and Children

Women traditionally attempt at hedging against low food availability by various means and tend to switch sources depending on the availability of food. As a consequence of the situation depicted by the 1993 and 1995 Food Calendars, women of the poor households are now required in 1995 to walk longer distances to collect whatever little food they can collect from the Secondary Food Security System than they were required of them earlier in 1993. With shrinkage in supply of such food, their capacity to hedge against food insecurity of their households was impaired in 1995. Given the intra-familial disparity and inequity in food consumption, the women including the girl child were likely to be subjected to even greater failure of food entitlements. However in 1998, due to the dispute in the tank (Rajbund) food from the Second Food System was again available to a limited extent, though not to the same extent as we saw in 1993.

It is common knowledge that the distribution of power within the households—like the distribution of food, is not always equitous. As a matter of fact within households, the eldest women wields the authority to allocate work amongst the women, the general principle of allocation being that the young and the agile are allocated those are that require highest expenditure of energy. Thus, the task of collecting food from CPRs was allocated to the younger women and girl children in the households. This meant that the girl children who worked to ensure food security for the family, had to forego their basic right of going to school. As a consequence, though Midnapore District had enjoyed the benefits of Total Literacy Campaign, the literacy level was poor and female illiteracy even more sharp.

The food calendar and the process of making it shows that the rural women, in general, are more proficient than rural men in depicting the variety of food which they generally collect from different sources. The variety of food available and the different sources of food are kept track of generally by the village women whether it is from ponds, river beds, forests, wild trees in the village and from nearby areas. It is they who are the principal actors in terms of collection of raw food, fruits, leaves, snails arid fishes for meeting food deficits in households (whether by eating less or supplementing their food consumption from other sources). The village women try to hedge against low food availability, and tend to switch sources depending on the seasons.

It is apparent as shown in the food calendars, that in some seasons more food is available in both quantity and variety such as in the month of 'Magh' (mid-January to mid-February), as compared to the, month of Aswin (mid-September to mid-October) when not much food is available from secondary sources. The concept of food security underlying the calendars is also remarkable. If attention is focused to columns 2, 3 and 4 of the seasonal food calendars, it is apparent that availability rice, potatoes and pulses provide the primary food security to the people, in the sense that these sources of food, are grown by the people by the application of technology (in the economic sense). Columns, 6, 7 and 8 of the seasonal food calendar indicate the Secondary Food Security available to the people, in the sense that food available from these sources are bestowed by nature (through the commons, forests, and wilderness) without any role for technology in production (again in the economic sense) at a time when primary food security is endangered. Significantly enough, the second hunger period (in the terminology of the 1993 Food Calendar) or the latter quarter of the long hunger period (in terms of the 1995 and the 1998 Food Calendars) is the harshest period of the year when even nature does not come to the rescue of the poor. Earlier researches have shown that in arid and semi-arid parts of the country the secondary food system could provide up to 33 per cent of the food requirement of the poor (see Jodha, 1993). Though weights of food generated from the Secondary Food System in the total consumption basket were not indicated in the Food Calendars, and such strong inference may not be appropriate, yet the significant role of the Secondary Food System even in high rainfall areas is ensuring food security for the poor is clearly brought out.

XII. Summary of Conclusions

Despite claims of "record food harvests" over the years, a burgeoning "buffer stock" of food, land the "supposed" growth in the economy percolating to the lowest unit of habitation benefiting the poor and resourceless households, hunger, both quantitatively and qaulitatively has increased in this village. The loss of "hunger food" generally and from common property resources in particular, have contributed towards elongating the hunger periods and robbed the poor households of a safety net provided by nature from the Secondary Food System. As real incomes decline over a fairly short period of time, food from secondary sources become scarce and employment opportunities shrink, the need to supplement familial income increases. If we examine the food security scenario over the years, that food availability had a critical role to play.

In months, following the harvests when food (rice and potatoes) availability is high, intake of food is high as well.

It is clear that in months, when people have work, that is, have purchasing power, they access food. And in seasons when employment opportunities are higher, namely in Aghrayan, Poush, Magh (the harvesting and post harvesting season) and in Ashar and Sravan (the cultivating season), the people also have higher food consumption. It is interesting that consumption levels peak when higher purchasing power is coupled with higher availability. That is consumption is determined by "income effect" and "quantity effect (price effect)" taken one with the other.

Rice, potatoes, fish, snails, sak (leafy vegetables) and meat are culturally acceptable food available to the people. The relative hunger of the people was in no way influenced by availability or otherwise of culturally acceptable food.

In terms of nutritional level, it is certain that the hunger periods are low on calorie intake and on nutritional value. The adequacy or otherwise of nutritional value could not be determined. Nonetheless, that the hunger would have been higher had there been no "backstopping" by food from the secondary system is quite clear.

If we examine the situation in terms of Sen's entitlement and deprivation thesis, it is clear that for the Lodha Tribe there is no "production based" entitlement as they are landless. There is no transfer entitlement, in any sense, particularly with the collapse of the PDS. There is no trade-based entitlement because these Lodha people do not possess any asset other than their labour, which they can trade for food.

The only entitlement to which the Lodha Tribe of Krishna Rakshit Chak is entitled to is "own labour entitlement," and were entitled to their own labour power and thus to the trade-based entitlements related to their labour power. That is the people of Krishna Rakshit Chak were entitled to whatever food they could have command over by exchanging their labour and because the people in Krishna Rakshit Chak operate in a market economy, they had exchange entitlements.

In case of Krishna Rakshit Chak, the exchange entitlement of the people was determined by:

(i) Ability to find employment and the duration thereof, which was highest in the months of Agrhayan, Poush and Magh (mid-November to mid-February), and to a more moderate extent during Ashar and Sravan (mid-June to mid-August).

(ii) The wages paid to them which were around Rs. 30 day plus a meal of puffed rice.

(iii) Ability to exchange their labour with nature (embodied in the CPRs) from which they acquired command over food.

(iv) By the cost of whatever food they brought which has lowest during the months succeeding other harvests and

(v) The indirect taxes that they are required to pay.

The exchange entitlement of the villagers of Krishna Rakshit Chak, were not determined by their ability to earn by selling their non-labour assets, as they had none, by the food that they could produce with their labour power and the resources they could buy and manage, because they had no land on which to grow food and their social security benefits, for they had none, except the PDS that operated at the margin and had also broken down.

In sum, the extent to which the people of Krishna Rakshit Chak were food secure, throughout the period 1993 to 1998, is a function of the exchange entitlement mapping that they face, they had no ownership of food. The people also faced food insecurity from 1995 onwards because of an unfavourable shift in exchange entitlement caused by rising food prices.

When queried about the character and content of their survival strategy, the poor villagers pointed out the assistance provided by the State in digging ponds for both irrigation and pisciculture. that the ponds were dug in 1994 and that those who were endowed with land could use water, helped the poorer community only marginally by helping those who had the resources, more particularly land. The need to devise programmes to support/augment the survival strategies for the landless and resourceless groups remains an area of major concern for the community.

The increase in food insecurity in village Krishna Rakshit Chak is a sad commentary on our reliance on the use of macro indicators to assess our National Food Security. Such indicators at the national level are often misleading to determine food security of the masses especially in areas of concentrated poverty. Krishna Rakshit Chak is just one village of the numerous cases where there persists chronic food-entitlement failure, despite the macro-indicators being favourable towards concluding that there is no apparent food insecurity in the country.

We have seen that the inflationary forces during 1994-95 have eroded the economic capacities of the tribal villagers to acquire food whether from the market or from the 'wild', in the absence of appropriate state interventions. Selective measures in terms of growing wild food on community lands, strengthening public distribution in such areas, creating opportunities for off-farm seasonal activities and provision of water and inputs for raising kitchen gardens can be useful steps in this context.

West Bengal has a system of Panchayats (locally elected self-government) and local level planning which has stabilished, despite criticisms and shortcomings. In such a scenario it is a lot easier to incorporate in the plan for state interventions to help the rural poor tackle their hunger, particularly so during the second hunger period (in terms of the 1993 Food Calendar) or the latter segment of the long hunger period of the 1995 and 1998 Food Calendars. There is already a scheme in the district sector for planting of fruit trees along roads and on common property resources. There is need to accelerate planting of fruit trees that bear fruits in the months of Aswin and Kartick. For instance, plantation of a late variety Mango (such as Kerwa mango in some parts of Eastern India) should be encouraged, particularly so because such variety of mango grow well in the soil and climate of the area under reference. Second, there is need to have a review on the public distribution system. The "hunger period" in the Months of Aswin and Kartick, being the period that coincides with the festive season of Bengal the supply of sugar, *Maida* (flour) and *Sooji* is customarily increased. It would be appropriate that during this period the government increases the supply of pulses and rice in the rural land ITDP areas, which would include villages like Krishna Rakshit Chak, more to tackle hunger than to meet festival consumption demand. Third, it could also be enjoined that during the said hunger period 'off-season' employment be provided by implementing more vigorously wage-employment generation schemes to shore up the income of the poor so that the poorer people have greater access to food, thereby preventing entitlement failure. Since these schemes are implemented by the Panchayats, it is possible to adjust them in order to tackle the problems of villages like Krishna Rakshit Chak. At a time when the State is being urged to retreat and it is fashionable to talk about letting the market forces deliver the goods, the importance of this element of State intervention can not be over-emphasized.

It is too well-known to be laboured here that the anti-poverty schemes are singularly gender insensitive and are top down. these need to be reversed, which is by no means difficult. For instance, participatory sessions with women villagers can be conducted to identify women-managed projects under such as plantation of trees and plants so as to increase food availability and decrease their hardship and uncertainty in collection of food. Practical suggestions can be sought from the village women not only for planting of plants and trees but more so for their maintenance in order to ensure sustainability. The women can be, empowered to collaborate in such projects in terms of their time and skills. Projects like wayside agro-forestry such as the one referred to earlier can also be taken up by rural women and can be managed by them exclusively, instead of restricting their share in wage employment up to a prescribed limit. The scope of such agro-forestry projects can be expanded to include seasonal plants whose flower, fruits, leaves, vegetables, roots and stems that can be used to supplement the food intake of the villagers. The time that would be saved by rural women in collection of food can be gainfully utilised by them in looking after such projects and sharing the return from such projects as they start flowing.

REFERENCES

Chambers Robert (1990), *Micro-environments Unobserved* (London: International Institute for Environment & Development), Gate Keeper Series.

Jodha, N.S. (1991), *Rural Common Property Resources: A Growing Crisis* (London: International Institute for Environment and Development).

Mukherjee, Amitava (1995), *Structural Adjustment Programme and Food Security in India* (Aldershot: Avebury).

Mukherjee, Amitava (1995-96), "Institutional Sanctions, Choice and the Secondary Food System: Incompleteness of Sen's Entitlement and Deprivation Thesis as an Explanation of Hunger," *Indian Economic Journal*, April-June.

Mukherjee, Neela (1997(b)), *Participatory Appraisal of Natural Resources* (Delhi: Concept Publishing Company).

Mukherjee, Neela and Mukherjee, Amitava (1994), "Rural Women and Food Insecurity: What a Food Calendar Reveals," *Economic and Political Weekly*, March 12.

Sen, Amartya (1981), *Poverty and Famines: An Essay in Entitlement and Failure* (Oxford: The Clarendon Press).

World Bank (1986), *The World Development Report* (Oxford: Oxford University Press).

3

PRA AND LIVESTOCK DEVELOPMENT IN INDIA
The Emerging Scenario

MAHESH CHANDER AND SANJAY KUMAR

Livestock development in India is going to receive much needed attention in the coming years owing to gradual recognition of its role in Indian economy. The contribution of livestock sub-sector to GDP within agricultural sector is increasing with the decline of agricultural sector's contribution in general to the national income. In the developed countries, agricultural sector's contribution is around 3-4 per cent while the livestock sub-sector within agricultural sector contributes over 50 per cent. The trend indicates that India too is moving in that direction and livestock sector is going to play a dominant and more visible role in Indian economy. India has already become number one milk producer in the world yet Indian livestock sector is vastly different than what it is in the developed countries where it is largely commercial. In India, 67 per cent of small, marginal and landless labourers own 70 per cent of all livestock. This group owns 90 per cent of small ruminant stock, and produces 76 per cent of milk and entire piggery sector is the virtual monopoly of the weaker sections of the society. 20 per cent of the eggs are also contributed by this group to the poultry industry dominated otherwise by the affluent farmers (Rao, 1997). As such, the Indian livestock sector needs attention entirely from the different perspective given its scope, dimensions and potential for national development.

India is enormous in terms of livestock population, diversity in species and breeds, feed and fodder resources, indigenous practices relating to livestock production and health care aspects yet the productivity as well as per capita availability of milk, meat, eggs is still very low in comparison to that of the developed countries. Nevertheless, improvements in these parameters are tremendous if we compare the figures at the time of India's independence and now, and relate this with the meagre attention paid to this sector including the financial allocation over the years. A comprehensive livestock development policy, which could take into account the grassroots realities of the livestock situation, is long felt yet not framed so far. Any sincere effort in this direction would therefore, call for taking stock of the scenario at the grassroots level across the country which has almost 15 agro-climatic zones with tremendous diversity in climate, topography, resources, customs, traditions, practices and potential. Here comes the role of Participatory Rural Appraisals (PRAs). No common strategy for whole of the country would work but the area specific approaches giving due recognition to the local conditions, requirements, perceptions, resource availability, traditions, practices and aspirations are needed. In doing so, PRAs could be of great help. This would ensure a bottom up approach to planning which has received a lot of attention in recent times. It is a question of managing the vast livestock resources in sustainable manner so as to reduce pressure on natural resources while ensuring food for ever growing vast human population in qualitative as well as quantitative terms.

PRA offers a creative approach to information sharing and a challenge to prevailing biases and pre-conceived notions about rural peoples' knowledge, aspirations and local situations. In spite of its potential merits, its application in livestock sector has been very limited so far in comparison to that in crop based farming activities. The available literature and case studies done clearly show an over-emphasis on PRA for crop production. Interestingly, the social scientists in agricultural universities and research institutions also hesitate in using PRAs to study livestock situation with the impression that PRAs are good for crop based farming activities only. This impression prevail so much so that PRAs in livestock production and health aspects have only a few examples given the vastness of livestock population (431.7 million, 15 per cent of world's livestock population) and dependence of Indian farming and farmers on it. This is one reason apart from the emerging role of livestock in Indian economy; this paper has dealt with some issues relating to PRA for livestock development in Indian context. In order to understand the role played by the livestock as a part of livelihood system for household survival in various communities, it is important to use appropriate PRA methods and techniques. The importance of PRA for livestock development has been well recognized at international level which is evident from the work done by several workers. The

International Institute for Environment and Development (IIED), UK has also published a special issue of RRA notes on livestock (IIED, 1994). This document obviously is a good guide for those who wish to work for the livelihood security through livestock development. An attempt has been made in this paper to make a case for PRA application in livestock development so as to augment its use in livestock management which at the moment is highly mismanaged system as is evident from the untapped potential of this giant sector.

PRA for livestock development was attempted by the authors as a part of a research project on, "Systems approach to livestock production and health delivery system in sub-Himalayan region" during 1997-99. Some of the basic methods of PRA were used in this project. For example, direct observation and village walks were used to assess the health and nutritional status of livestock, the housing system, grazing and feeding strategy, care of calf, members of family involved with the livestock management activities/gender role etc. In general, this helped in developing a general idea of the livestock rearing in the region which was an important precursor to the much detailed investigation through other PRA methods and techniques at a later stage. It is important to have an idea of the local farming system as much possible and in doing so, PRA has no match. The direct observation and village walks including the transacts are the easiest and least time consuming methods for learning about the local livestock management and production system including identifying the key indicators. While doing PRA for livestock issues, the fact was accepted that as such, there is no standard PRA for livestock but the available methods and techniques of PRA were attempted to study the livestock issues as well. The available literature (Mukherjee, 1993; IIED, 1994 and Mukherjee, 1995) served as good guide to conduct the PRA in the selected villages. With the growing use of PRA, the methods can be further streamlined for use in livestock issues in future.

The direct observation alongwith informal questioning resulted in a substantial amount of general and specific information, hence proved to be an important tool while conducting the PRA. In hills, farmers let loose their livestock particularly cattle and goats in morning till afternoon for grazing in the nearby forest or harvested fields. That is the right time to have a look on the livestock types and their general health. Such livestock move in-groups and pass through the village and thus, give good opportunity for observation. This is followed by a walk through the village which gives an idea about the housing system, feed and fodder availability in the village and feeding strategies adopted by the villagers, care of the young stock, etc. The farm household map, flow diagram and technology map for animals (Figs. 31, 3.2 and 3.3) were prepared for the villages under study which gave enough insight about the villages studied. All those functionaries who are responsible for livestock development in a given area would find it an important first step to understand the local livestock management system including the role played by men and women in various activities related to livestock management.

The technology map for animals (Fig. 3.3), for example, was drawn after a thorough transact within the neighbourhood of the village to identify the technology related to livestock adopted by the farmers. Here we also discussed the problems faced by the farmers in adopting the particular technology. In this typical hill village (Sunarkhola), only a few improved technologies related to livestock were visible. The Artificial Insemination(AI) was a technology rejected by the farmers owing to low conception rate, feeding of concentrate was practiced but only to milking animals, whereas, vaccination to animals was forced rejection due to lack of veterinary facilities. Poultry and rabbit rearing was adopted in recent past but later discontinued due to high mortality and lack of proper veterinary care. This was a typical case of disenchantment discontinuation. Colestrum feeding to new born calf was the technology adopted by the farmers. As such, the technology map drawn with the help of the farmers can give enough insight about the technology adopted, rejected and discontinued.

PRAs often bring out harsh realities as well that prevail at grassroots levels. For example, cross-breeding in cattle involving exotic breeds has been attempted in hill region since 1960s by many agencies including foreign, national, NGOs and cooperatives. The result is indicates obvious negligible impact so far. Only about 5 per cent of cattle are cross-bred in the region which again are relatively less productive owing to several constraints like low feed and fodder availability, high susceptibility to diseases and poor adaptability to local situations and requirements. The Matrix score ranking done in the selected villages revealed preferences of the farmers for the livestock species in the order: buffalo, goat, local cow and lastly cross-bred cow (Table 3.1). The cross-bred cow stood last owing to its non-suitability given the local scarcity situation prevailing in a typical rain-fed and mountainous terrain with its obvious constraints. The poor performance of cross-breeding programmes in central Himalayan region has also been discussed alongwith the reasons for the failure by several workers through their empirical studies (Singh, 1994a; Singh, 1998; Chander, 1997). Moreover, the energy efficiency of cross-

FIG. 3.1: Household Map of Mr. R.D. Kholia

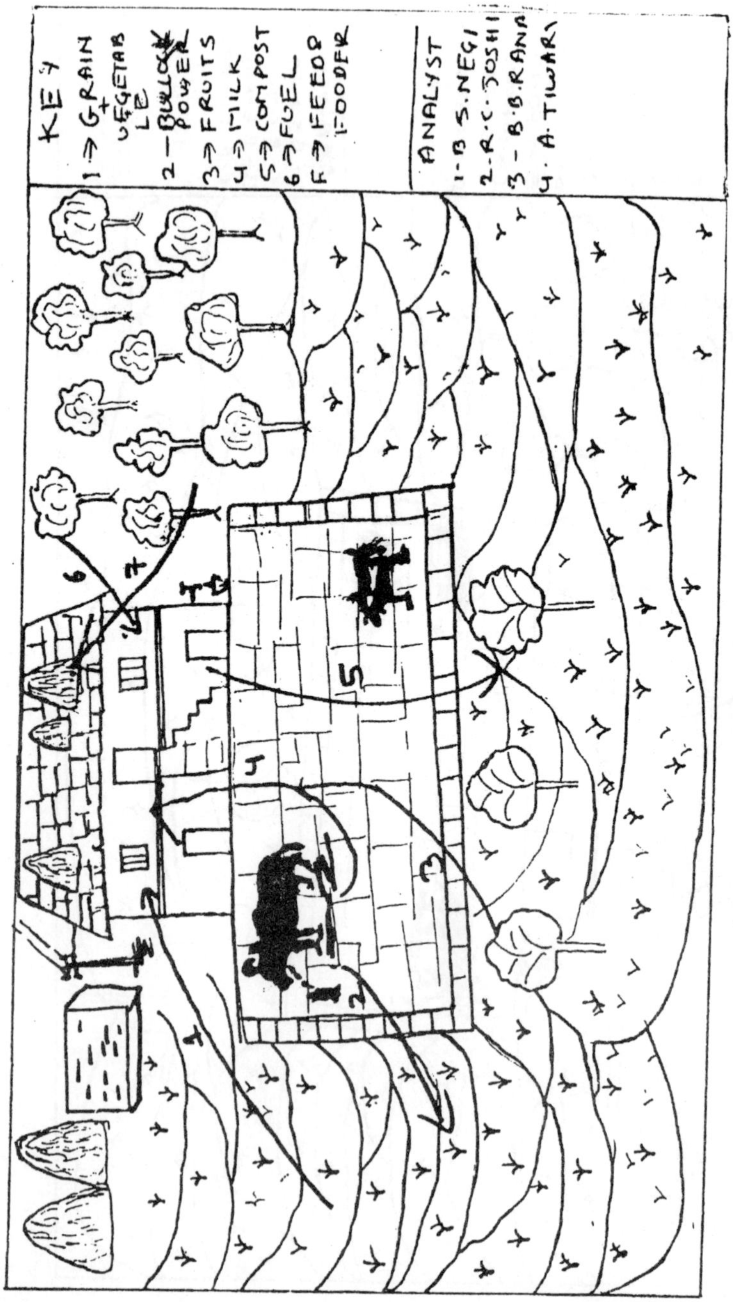

FIG. 3.2: Resourse Flow Diagram

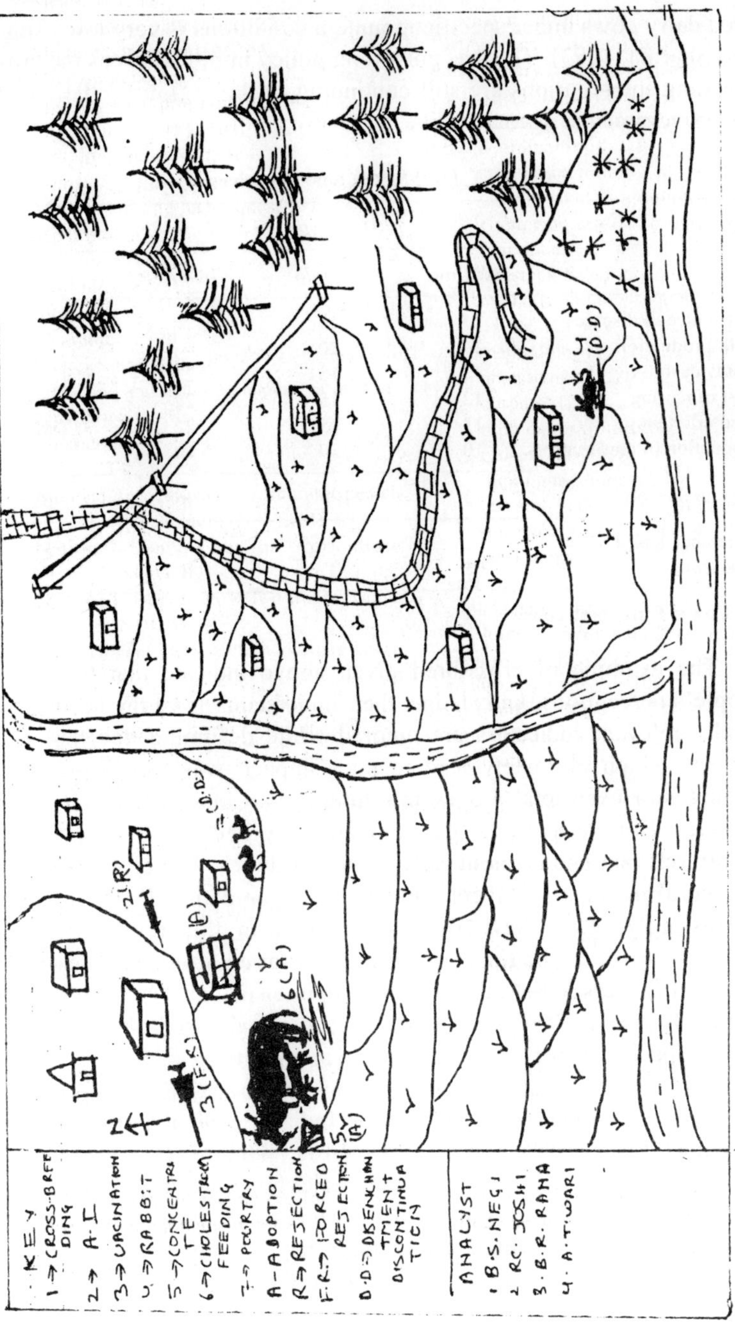

FIG. 3.3: Technology Map of Village Sonar Khola-Dankanya

bred dairy cows under specific mountain conditions is very low (Singh and Sharma, 1993). This has got strong policy implications as the cross breeding interventions are still continuing in the region by the NGOs and governmental agencies alike.

TABLE 3.1: Final Matrix Score for Livestock

Attributes	*Type of Livestock*			
	Hill Cow	*Buffalo*	*Goat*	*CB Cow*
Resistance to disease	15	17	20	11
Milk production	13	20	—	13
Ready cash	12	15	22	10
Cost of rearing	12	15	22	10
Feed efficiency	13	15	22	12
Production of cow dung	10	20	10	12
Total rank score	75	103	96	68
Preference based on rank score	III	I	II	IV

CB Cow = Cross-bred cow

The example of cross-bred given above indicate that the local people's perceptions, knowledge, their understanding of the needs and locally relevant indicators are ignored while designing development projects which ultimately lead to poor impact, wastage of precious resources or even total programme failure with loss of faith on these agencies. Buffalo and goat got comparatively better score due to the locally relevant and economically viable attributes. The census figures also confirm the rise in goat and buffalo population in the region. Interestingly, goats have risen in number in this region despite discouragement by the financial institutions for environmental reasons. The local farmers do not subscribe to the opinion that goat is environment unfriendly animal. To them, goat is very economical, sustainable livestock animal species fit for rearing in the local conditions of low feed and fodder besides the cash crunch problem with the majority of the small and marginal farmers who dominate in India in general and in hills in particular. The farmers believe that man is far more responsible than goat for that matter any other livestock species for environmental damage. This indicates that farmers make their own choices and decisions based on ground realities which affect their day to day life unlike the governmental agencies which often ignore their conventional wisdom and understanding of the local issues, needs and requirements. Here, PRAs play pivotal role in bringing forth the farmers perspectives, which needs to be incorporated in the development strategies. Women's participation has been particularly ignored at formal level though they do almost all the activities relating to livestock management. The ethno-veterinary wisdom of hill women was found to be amazing yet very poorly documented, unrecognized, un-rewarded and made inconsequential in the formal paradigms of development. It is important to crystalize that who is researching for whom, who is participating in what activities with what potential benefits.

In the course of PRA exercise, farmers' choices/preferences for fodder trees and grasses were also studied through matrix score ranking method. The results presented in Table 3.2 and Table 3.3 indicate that farmers were very clear about their choices which were based on the locally relevant criteria decided by the farmers themselves like round

TABLE 3.2: Final Matrix Score for Fodder Tree Species

Attributes	*Type of Fodder Tree*					
	Kharsu	*Dudhila*	*Kharik*	*Bhimal*	*Banj*	*Padam*
Palatable to animal	11	22	14	26	10	15
Round the year fodder	15	23	16	20	17	14
Increases the milk production	11	10	10	28	21	19
Leaves used as bedding material	23	8	13	10	25	9
Multipurpose use of the tree	24	20	13	19	20	15
Total rank score	84	83	66	103	93	72
Preference based on rank score	III	IV	VI	I	II	V

TABLE 3.3: Final Matrix Score for Fodder Grass Species

Attributes	*Type of Fodder Grass*					
	Kumeria	*Bimosia*	*Doob*	*Kans*	*Babila*	*Chalmoda*
Palatable to animals	18	18	13	16	23	17
Increases the milk yield	20	18	16	19	15	7
No. of cuttings	16	27	24	15	13	10
Suitability for hay making	14	27	19	15	18	12
Soil conservation properties	18	25	16	16	13	17
Total rank score	86	125	88	81	82	63
Preference based on rank score	III	I	II	V	IV	VI

the year availability, palatability, quick growth, multi-cut possibility, length of grass, multi-purpose uses, milk enhancing ability, soil conservation capability, survival ability under adverse climatic conditions. Unfortunately, these local grasses and fodder trees so far have not found place in the grass and fodder development policies and programmes including the social forestry projects initiated in this region. The concerned agencies are still mesmerized with the idea of so called improved grasses, which have very poor adaptability in local rain-fed situations. Moreover, the farmers of the region owing to their small land holdings are less inclined to grow grasses and fodder. These farmers prefer to depend on naturally growing local grasses along the bunds, uncultivated less fertile land, forest areas, etc. where the improved grasses and fodder can't grow owing to their dependence on inputs. Whereas, the local grasses due to high adaptability to local rain-fed situation grow abundantly and luxuriantly. This calls for giving due importance to local situations and farmer's wisdom about their farming conditions, which has been accumulated over the years. More attention is required to be paid to the native grasses and fodder trees by formulating strategies to improve the nutritive values, palatability and growth potential. The choice/preferences of farmers can be obtained for many other indicators as well which empower the farmers in a way that they decide the things, which have implications for their livelihoods. The developmental agencies may bear in mind the preferences of farmers as well as the local conditions while designing the developmental interventions for different regions.

PRAs have several potential uses in livestock sector development *viz.* livestock population assessment through livestock mapping, distribution of livestock per household (by social mapping), livestock preferences in a community, documenting indigenous knowledge and ethno-veterinary practices, estimation of mortality, morbidity, and nutritional status of livestock in a given region, proportional income from livestock products, resources available to livestock (through seasonal resource mapping), feed and fodder preferences, modes and sources of acquisition and disposal of livestock, the perceived status of livestock in relation to other assets, resource analysis for livestock production, livestock diseases and other health issues. Some of the applications of PRA in these areas have been documented (Kirsopp-Reed, 1994). The methods and techniques of PRA for livestock development are gradually finding place in the research and training programmes of national level institutions with the scope for further applications at regional or local level institutions. The field veterinarians posted in the hill districts of Uttar Pradesh were enquired through a mailed questionnaire survey about their interest and need of training in the area of FSR and PRA. They expressed the need for training on PRA and FSR methods and techniques alongwith the refresher courses in their professional fields (Chander, *et al.*, 1998). This is indicative of the rising interest in PRA among the field veterinarians as well. An overview of the PRA application in livestock sector has been presented to describe the emerging scenario in Indian context.

PRA and Livestock: An Overview

National Academy of Agricultural Research Management (NAARM), Hyderabad is one good source for disseminating the concepts like FSR, On-Farm research and PRAs as it impart training to a large number of agricultural scientists of Indian Council of Agricultural Research (ICAR) as well as in-service training to the teachers of the agricultural universities. The fresh Agricultural Research Service (ARS) Scientists of ICAR undergo six months induction training at NAARM (Foundation Course for Agricultural Research Service (FOCARS). The Field Experience Training (FET) which is an essential feature of the NAARM training, has PRA at its core of training content. The scientists undertake the FET in villages in different agro-ecological zones of the country. Livestock being the integral component of the Indian mix farming system, is gradually attracting the attention of the scientists including the PRAs used to study it. The FET reports submitted by the trainees of different batches to the NAARM reveal that a good number of studies are being undertaken on livestock farming systems in addition to the focus on the crop production issues. These scientists on their regular postings in different ICAR institutes further disseminate these concepts apart from being themselves the potential users of PRA methods and techniques while undertaking the research projects.

National Dairy Research Institute (NDRI), Karnal in Haryana is one of the pioneering ICAR institutes which has successfully used RRA/PRA in livestock sector. The Indo-Dutch project on Bio-conversion of crop residues (BIOCON) which started in 1985 by ICAR in collaboration with the Wageningen Agricultural University (The Netherlands) and Winrock International, used RRAs/PRA as a strategy to understand the farmers' perspective in relation to straw feeding to animals. In this particular project, straw feeding has been considered as a typical systems issue where several disciplines meet *viz.* Animal nutrition, crop science, sociology, economics, plant breeding, gender and FSR specialists. This was a unique project in a sense that systems perspective was kept in mind while collecting the data from across the agro-climatic zones of the country with PRA/RRA methods and techniques used prominently (Singh, 1994; Singh and Schiere, 1994; Singh and Schiere, 1995; De Boer, *et al.*, 1994). Apart from NDRI, BAIF (Pune), National Dairy Development Board (NDDB), Anand and Indian Grassland and Fodder Research Institute (IGFRI), Jhansi has applied PRA methods to study livestock farming systems as partners in the BIOCON project. These are a few illustrations where PRA has not only been accepted as the appropriate methodology but also extensively used to study the various dimensions of the livestock farming system.

In World Bank financed projects or for that matter any other donor funded development schemes like watershed management projects, concepts like FSR, On-Farm research and PRA are invariably emphasized. For instance, Uttar Pradesh Diversified Agricultural Support Project (UPDASP)—a World Bank assisted project currently under implementation in Uttar Pradesh, has livestock development as one of the important component where PRA is being used as one of the essential feature for designing livestock development strategy. This is one positive development as far as application of PRA is concerned for livestock development. The FSR approaches though have emphasis on holistic studies and as such it is difficult to study livestock component in isolation given the mixed nature of Indian agriculture yet there is scope for using PRAs to exclusively study livestock component within broad mixed farming system as it exists in India unlike in developed countries where specialized livestock enterprises are pre-dominant. PRAs are gradually being accepted as one of the important tools for data generation and more so as a means of understanding the grassroots realities holistically. The livestock sector with its gradual emergence and bright prospects for future can not afford to neglect the potential applications of PRAs. As such, many workers and institutions are using it and its application is likely to find even better place in livestock development policies and programmes in future. Some of the examples given here are indicative of the trends and certainly not exhaustive.

Concluding Remarks

We learnt after spending considerable time with the villagers that we have to unlearn a lot. In particular, we needed to rethink, refine what we had learnt through generalized nature of our academic curriculum which had taught us the science of agriculture in general. The PRA experience taught us how to combine and match the academic knowledge with that of the local situations and requirements. In the course of the research project, we used questionnaire surveys, interviews, RRAs/PRAs which gave us understanding of the merits and limitations of these methods. The PRAs obviously helped us far more in changing our traditional mindset and preconceived notion about the modern technologies including biases for example, for A.I. The old and young, children and women, all have their own thoughts, problems, and solutions which need to be shared through methods like PRA.

Here we consider imperative to highlight the views of an aged farmer from Ghotia village in Padampuri area of Nainital district, about rapidly growing floriculture industry in his area. In his opinion, farmers who are leasing out their land for floriculture to the entrepreneurs who are mostly outsiders, are doing wrong to their coming generations . He says, may be the current earning would appear to be very high but in few years, the land would be depleted of the fertility as the floriculturists were not using Farm Yard Manure (FYM)—an essential feature of hill farming, but depending on heavy doses of chemical fertilizers for quick returns. The exotic flowers like Geranium, Lillium, Gladiolus grown in controlled environment are being exported from the area. He apprehends, after sometime, these entrepreneurs might move to some other areas given their resourcefulness, leaving the local farmers in the lurch. He further says, the ready cash income often paid in advance disappear fast in reckless spending by the poor local farmers in celebrations and non-economic activities. This further adds to the drudgery of the hill women as their menfolk enjoy for sometime with the easy cash with them. In long run, he says, it will be disastrous decision to lease out the land to the outsiders for activities like floriculture. According to him, hill farming can not survive without livestock and those farming practices which exclude livestock (large scale floriculture as being practiced in the area, for example) would not be sustainable from the point of local farmers. Here it has not been argued that floriculture *per se* is bad but some farmers based on their conventional wisdom and experiences have their opinion against the kind of floriculture being initiated in the area. One has to learn how best one can take into consideration or at least respect such type of views which are otherwise quite often contrary to the established knowledge disseminated from the Agricultural Universities, Research and Development Institutions. The authors owing to their academic qualifications in agriculture would have immediately opposed or criticized the views of the farmer talking against commercial floriculture or cross-breeding interventions. However, for their exposure to new development paradigms including PRA methods, they had to consider the views though contrary to their knowledge acquired through formal qualifications.

The case of floriculture has been cited to emphasise that one has to learn what is important from the local point of view besides being important from the standpoint of modernization as well as commercialization of agriculture. The local point of view need to be strengthened through PRAs involving multi-disciplinary teams and local farmers. The livestock farming system in hills supplement and complement to the crop farming system and as such, is an essential feature of the hill small holder agriculture. Similarly, the livestock may be playing different roles in different agro-climatic zones which need to be studied through PRA methods and techniques. The current paper is only a small attempt to make a case for PRA application in livestock sector management in India in particular. The country wide PRAs, if done to study the livestock farming system, would help in framing a sustainable livestock development policy for the country.

REFERENCES

Chander, Mahesh (1997), "PRA and Participatory Extension: Theory, Practice and Implications." In: Neela Mukherjee, Vinita Kumar, Meera Jayaswal, Bratindi Jena (eds), *Learning to Share (Experiences and Reflections on PRA and Community Participation)*,New Delhi, Concept Publishing Company, pp. 23-34.

Chander, Mahesh; Kumar, Sanjay; Harbola, P.C. and Dey, A. (1998), *Systems Approach to Livestock Health and Production System in Mountainous Region of India: Some Preliminary Observations of a Research Project*, Proc. 15th International Symposium of the AFSR-E, Vol. 2, Pretoria (South Africa), November 29th-4 December, pp. 1038-41.

De Boer, A.J.; Singh, C.B.; Dixit, P.K.; Lotan Singh; Patil, B.R. (1994), *Rapid Rural Appraisals to assist focussing of Research and Extension Programmes for Livestock Development in India*, Technical Publication No. 2, ICAR/BIOCON/Winrock International, Kiran Singh and J.B. Schiere (series editors),Indian Council of Agricultural Research, Krishi Bhawan, New Delhi, p. 46.

"IIED" (1994), Special Issue on Livestock, *RRA Notes No. 20*. London, IIED, p. 165.

Kirshopp-Reed, Kate (1994), "A Review of PRA Methods for Livestock Research and Development." In: *RRA Notes No. 20*, Special Issue on Livestock, London, IIED, pp. 11-36.

Mukherjee, Neela (1993), *Participatory Rural Appraisal: Methodology and Applications*, New Delhi, Concept Publishing Company, p. 159.

Mukherjee, Neela (1994), "Livestock, Livelihood and Drought: A PRA Exercise in Botswana." In: Special issue on livestock, *RRA Notes No. 2*, London, IIED, pp. 127-29.

Mukherjee, Neela)1995), *Participatory Rural Appraisal and Questionnaire Survey (Comparative Field Experience and Methodological Innovations)*, New Delhi, Concept Publishing Company, p. 163.

Rao, C.K. (1997), "Livestock in India—Instruments of Social Justice" (Dr. V.S. Alwar Memorial Oration), *Indian Veterinary Journal*, 74, 7, pp. 11-22.

Singh, C.B. (1994), *Rapid Rural Appraisal for Identification of Problems and Opportunities in Dairy Farming Systems*, Proc. of All India Dairy Husbandry Officers Workshop, Karnal, NDRI, Dec. 2-3.1993, pp. 69-75.

Singh, Kiran and J.B. Schiere (1994), "On-farm Research for Testing of Appropriate Technologies in Crop Livestock Production Systems." ICAR/BAIF/BIOCON/ Winrock International, *Technical Bulletin No. 3*, ICAR, New Delhi and Wageningen Agricultural University, The Netherlands.

Singh, Kiran and J.B. Schiere (eds.) (1995), *Handbook for Straw Feeding Systems (Principles and Application with Emphasis on Indian Livestock Production)*, ICAR, New Delhi and Wageningen Agricultural University, The Netherlands.

Singh, Vir (1994a), "Cross Breeding An Utter Failure," *Financial Express*, New Delhi, 20 July.

Singh, Vir (1998), "Draught Animal Power in Mountain Agriculture (A Study of Perspectives and Issues in the Central Himalayas, India), *Mountain Farming Systems Discussion Paper Series No. MFS98/1*, Kathmandu, International Centre for Integrated Mountain Development (ICIMOD), p. 152.

Singh, Vir and Sharma, R.J. (1993), "Energetics of Cross-bred Dairy Cows in Himalayan Environment," In Vir Singh (Ed), *Eco Crisis in the Himalaya: Causes, Consequences and Way Out*, Dehradun, IBD, pp. 147-16.

4

EVOLVING PROCESS OF PEOPLE'S PARTICIPATION IN FORESTRY
A Review of Experience in Rajasthan

ABHIJIT GHOSE

Introduction

People's participation has become the buzz word in all developmental processes in modern world. It has been realised that unless the people, who are the ultimate beneficiaries of the developmental process, are actively involved, the development process may not be sustainable over long run. A welfare-oriented Government committed for development of its citizens may take up any programme with all sincerity but if people are not involved it is most likely to end up as a typical governmental programme. There are innumerable examples of success stories in people's participation in various sectors of development round the globe and over a period of nearly two decades, participation of people have evolved in the forestry sector of India in a slow and steady manner.

It is a well-known fact that forest degradation in India has happened in an accelerated pace due to enormous anthropogenic pressure particularly in the post independent era. All efforts made by Forest Department (FD) to save forests from further degradation came up as a conflict of interest with local population, who are basically dependent on these forests for their subsistence living. Though national interest was paramount to local interest, the dwindling forest resources suggested that without a paradigm shift in management of forests, existence of forests can not be guaranteed to future generations.

Forests have three major roles to play in the society—ecological, protective and productive. Although there was no controversies regarding ecological and protective roles, the productive role of forests was misconstrued in the traditional silvicultural practices in terms of emphasis on timber. In reality, a small size of human population has demand for timber, while a vast majority of people are dependent on small timber, firewood and fodder for their day to day subsistence living. Poor and marginalized people who remain in the close vicinity of forests usually go to forests to gather their food, firewood and fodder besides number of Non-Timber Forest Products (NTFPs) like medicinal herbs, floss and fibres, etc. In 1976, National Commission on Agriculture (NCA) in its epoch making report had emphasized the need of social forestry *vis-a-vis* production forestry. Production forestry puts emphasis on timber and related industrial raw materials, while social forestry lays emphasis on those varieties of products which are in great demand in society for meeting their daily subsistence needs. NCA in its report also suggested that all government wastelands in form of linear strips available along roads, canals, railway lines and other wastelands be available as compact blocks in possession of the government or local communities with massive plantations to meet the needs of the society mainly in form of firewood, small timber and fodder. Since these plantations are to be raised near habitations, NCA report envisaged that while raising these plantations local people should be taken into confidence and actively involved in their development. Since then foresters who alienated themselves from the local people in the process of usual discharge of their duty on forest protection by imposing all kinds of prohibitive orders, started with difficulty to redefine their role in the changing scenario.

Historical Perspective

People's participation in the forestry was never a myth. In a State like Rajasthan, there were rich traditions and indigenous practices for conservation and natural resource management. Sacred groves of trees in name of 'Dev Vans' or 'Orans' are of common occurrence in the entire state from hills to the core of deserts. Therefore, practices like 'Kesar Chhanta' where ethnic communities of tribal move around a patch of forest beating drums and simultaneously sprinkling flowers for their sacred deities, so that none dare remove even a twig from such area. The supreme sacrifice of 360 men and women to save 'Khejri' tree at Khejedli village near Jodhpur almost 300 years back is a reminder of the sage of unparallel instance of nature conservation by people. People of Vishnoi community still live in desert pockets even today, and never hesitate to sacrifice their lives for conservation of flora and fauna.

Community Woodlots

With the advent of socio forestry in Rajasthan, major breakthrough came while raising community woodlots on village common lands. In initial years when village communities like Panchayats were approached by Forest Department (FD) staff, not many Panchayats were keen to part their lands to FD as they were very apprehensive about getting lands back as promised to them and they looked upon it as an evil design of government to establish control over their 'Charagaha' or 'Gochar' lands earmarked for common grazing. FD officials managed to convince few of these Panchayats and raised successful plantations on them. Grasses which came in the interspace of tree crops first year onwards were given to villagers free of cost to cut and carry. More and more Panchayats came forward after a mutual building up of trust. Raising of community woodlots on village common land got an impetus while large scale plantations were raised under centrally sponsored schemes like Desert Development Programmes launched in desert districts funded by World Bank and USAID. National Social Forestry Project was launched in rest of the 16 non-desert districts. Many successful plantations of community woodlots not only succeeded to remove mistrust between community and FD, but also rich assets were created and transferred to village communities. During the process, FD's action was under active scrutiny by NGO groups and others who became very vocal critic of all such activities. Due to ever increasing cattle to man ratio, costly fencing were raised in the beginning with angle irons and barbed wire to protect plantations but slowly FD could persuade communities to keep away their livestocks. In the later years of establishment from such woodlots, either fencing was not done at all or notional fencing were erected in few plantations for demarcation purposes. Such fencing were popularly termed as "social fencing." Although there were provisions to handover developed woodlots back to Panchayats, in certain areas Panchayats were reluctant to take possession as they feared that with weak legal support it would be impossible to protect those assets when FD would withdraw themselves from physical protection.

Till the end of the Eighth Five year Plan, more than 1,10,000 ha. of community woodlots were created all over the state. Most woodlots after maintenance period were handed over to respective Panchayats for further management. However, the response has been mixed as regards maintenance of such assets. At places due to ineffective control of Panchayats, created assets have been destroyed. But in many places,

Panchayats have augmented their income by selling lops and tops of standing trees and have created successful examples for emulation.

People's Involvement

In raising of community woodlots, Forest Department (FD) has secured people's participation to a great extent but in reality such participation is far from complete. The work is taken up with the consent of Panchayats but it can not be taken as total consensus of villagers. Various categories of people get themselves involved at different periods of development. At the beginning, Sarpanch and other members those who are influential in society get involved in proposing land to FD. Later wage earners among village community get involved when FD starts various activities of fencing, soil work and actual planting and their subsequent maintenance. Since work involved are not of tough nature and worksites are usually closer to village, 50 to 60 per cent labour employees constitute poor women. When grasses come and FD permits cut and carry of grass on 'first come first serve' basis, again women who rear cattle come for this purpose and men who have large livestock also come forward for grass cuttings. Again women collect dry fallen wood for the purpose of cooking. Whenever harvesting is done wage labour is involved and finally during sharing of produce a larger section of village communities get involved. In the planting, mostly FD's choice of species were final but now whenever discussions are held for harvesting and replanting many villagers opine for better species of their choice. Preparation of management plan and formation of protection committees are relatively new development.

Although participation approaches were adopted in plantations on community lands and other government lands, participatory approach in raising of plantations or protection of forest lands were not initiated until new forest policy of 1988 was announced. This policy was a complete departure from the earlier policy of 1952 in many respects. The new policy outlined its main approach as one of people's participation in protection, conservation and management of forests.

Paradigm Change

Realising the symbiotic relationship between forest which is considered in India as the largest community resource and the indigenous inhabitants including marginalised people living within and near the forests, 1988 forest policy states that:

* The villagers' customary rights and concessions should be fully protected.
* Their domestic requirements of fuelwood, fodder, Non-Timber Forest Produce (NTFP) and small timber should be the first charge on forest produce.
* Their income and employment should be enhanced by improving and increasing the production of NTFPs, and
* That a "massive people's movement with the involvement of women," should be created for achieving the policy objectives.

Thus there has been a complete reversal of earlier priorities of forest management which was tilted towards timber primacy and commercial exploitation of forests. Local needs are of paramount importance rather than meeting needs of industries for raw materials. To translate the new policy into action the Ministry of Environment and Forests, Government of India issued detailed guidelines for all State and Union Territories Governments on 1st June, 1990 to "involve village communities and Voluntary Agencies in the regeneration of degraded forests." In line with these guidelines, Government of Rajasthan issued a resolution on 15th March, 1991 to involve village communities in the regeneration of degraded forests. On 26th April, 1991, a similar set of resolution was brought out by the State Government to involve village communities in plantations raised on degraded lands owned by the government as well as community. The State Government also decided to take up all forestry activities in the State with active involvement of local people. In compliance of this decision, so far 2705 Village Forest Protection and Management Committees have been formed to develop 2.35 lakh ha. of degraded forests and non-forest land. Now the villagers are realising that forests belong to them and they should play a very active role in managing their own forests. With constant interactions between villagers and officials of FD, such role clarity has became focused. So far FD officials did not care to consult local people about development of forests and at the same time local people were thinking protection and management of forests are not their responsibilities. But through this process, both FD staff and villagers realised that management of forests is collective responsibility of both sides and the new era of Joint Forest Management has dawned.

Joint Forest Management

Since the concept of Joint Forest Management (JFM) is in a evolving phase, FD staff are required to take considerable initiative to make their intentions clear to villagers. At grass-roots level of FD, number of training programmes and motivational camps are organised for explaining and communicating reversal of their roles. FD staff before taking up any development activities take local villagers into confidence and give them relevant information of Joint Forest Management resolution. Majority of the village adults then take a decision to form a Village Forest Protection and Management Committee (VFPMC) and choose a suitable person as Chairperson of the Executive Committee. Local forest staff act as member secretary of the committee who not only convenes meeting of Executive Committee but maintains regular proceedings of such meeting. The staff also takes up lead role in preparing micro-plan of village by adopting technique of Participatory Rural Appraisal (PRA). Subsequent development activities are taken up as per micro-plan.

Execution of development activities are undertaken by FD staff employing labour from the village. But since 1996, the State Government has launched an innovative scheme of Janata Van Yojna where the VFPMC is sufficiently empowered to take up execution, FD would transfer funds to VFPMC who can execute the work with technical support from the FD staff. So far atleast 100 to 120 VFPMCs have taken up Janata Van Yojna scheme in entire state. After planting operation is over, from the very first year grasses come up and VFPMC decides how and in what manner disposal of grass and other minor forest products are to be done. In most of the cases token money is kept for issuing permit of cut and carry of grass. This money is kept in a separate bank account. If grass production is more than the need of the villagers it is sold and in such cases sale proceed is deposited in the committee's account. Many committees also levy a token fee of membership from participatory households and deposit the same in their bank account. Wage labourers of the village are persuaded to part with a portion of wage for committee's fund. The generated funds are utilised for various development activities as per microplan prepared and it is known as Village Development Fund (VDF). Treasurer of the executive committee keeps up the record of all cash transactions. At certain places if committee members violate rules, e.g., indulge in illicit grazing or felling, committee realises fines as punishment which goes in the common funds. However, if someone other than committee members indulge in illicit activities, committee members handover such offenders to FD staff for legal action. In order to encourage communities in forest protection in certain areas of tribal belts of the State where FD is implementing schemes like World Food Programme, out of the generated funds VFPMCs have taken up certain activities like installing of hand pump in the village, constructing approach road to village, mid-day meal programmes in village primary school, constructing of community hall, constructing a *puca* raised platform in village centre, constructing of anicuts for minor irrigation, etc., known as Entry Point Activities. A part of fund is donated either in cash or in kind (*sramdan*) by VFPMC. In most of such cases VFPMC had taken initiative to use VDF for tangible work. A VFPMC named Bhanpurkalan in Amer (Jaipur) has donated Rs. 30,000 from their village development fund, a NGO called Tarun Bharat Sangh of Thanagaji gave Rs. 40,000 and villages contributed voluntary labour worth Rs. 5000 to construct a big earthen dam to store water in Bhanpurkalan at a total outlay of Rs. 75,000. After two seasons of its construction, many villagers have said that it helped immensely in recharging of their wells located in the downstream of earthen dam. Thus it is an ideal example where activities like plantations could result in such snowballing effect on village development.

It is also amazing to find that a VFPMC called Datier in Chittorgarh district is engaged in protection of 1100 ha. of degraded forests of Teak by collective effort. Villagers by turn move in a group for patrolling around forests. They belong to tribal communities. The State Government recognizing their contribution for forest protection, awarded them Amrita Devi Award by giving a cash prize of Rs. 50,000 besides citation. Salukhera VFPMC of Udaipur district have raised 200 ha. plantation on degraded forest lands between 1993 to 1996 and religiously protected these forests. Grass is now abundantly available and villagers sold off their goats and sheep and instead brought milch cows and buffaloes and stall feed them. In 1997, they started pisciculture. Out of the generated funds in World Food Programme, few women of the village were imparted training in sewing and sewing machines were distributed to these trained women. By such skill upgradation, their income got supplemented. This VFPMC was awarded Indira Priyadarshini Vrikhamitra Award at the national level with a cash prize of Rs. 50,000 alongwith a citation. Wherever local staff take interests, VFPMCs are doing exemplary work.

Performance Indicator

Out of the more than two thousands VFPMCs formed so far about 50 per cent committees are found to be in "very active" or "active" categories. Performance indicators of successful committees are not yet standardised but some of the parameters can be taken for drawing selected inferences. From the status of forests/plantations, number of reported forest offenses, production of grasses etc., health of forests can be judged. Similarly, number of people who attend meetings, number of meetings held, proceedings of meetings, number of different groups of members attending meeting proportionate to their population of village are certain social indicators. Similarly, the amount of deposit in Village Development Fund (VDF), sharing modalities for different products, quantum of grasses received *vis-a-vis* total demand, increase of family income are certain economic indicators for a well managed committee. Leadership qualities of Chairperson, number of conflicts occurred and number of such conflicts resolved during the year are some of the qualitative indicators of functioning of committees. In majority of such committees role of women is marginal because in a men dominated society, women members are rarely consulted while *purdah* system are still prevalent among certain castes. However in tribal areas, women do express opinion amidst their men counterparts. NGOs are considered as cementing force between government agencies and villagers. But since majority of NGOs have weak-base in rural areas, participation of NGOs are also inconspicuous.

New Resolution

At the beginning, there were no adequate experience about people's participation, resolution issued by Government was silent in many issues. After thorough deliberation and consultation with various stake holders, a new resolution was brought out in May, 1999 which replaced resolution of 15th March, 1991. In order to increase women's participation, in the new resolution now each household were to have two adult members out of which one should be woman for each VFPMC. In order to further assure women's representation, a sub-committee is suggested for women only. One of the vocal woman is to be made Chairperson of that sub-committee, Similarly, in the executive body consisting of 11 members, it is mandatory to have 3 women members and out of them one should be Chairperson of women sub-committee. The local forester is to be made the member secretary to start with but if some educated person of the village is willing, in two years time such person can be made member secretary. When a forester is made member secretary, she will have no voting rights but a non-official can be given voting rights. Official members are not given voting rights but they are inducted as facilitators. Other important highlights of the amended resolution are as follows:

* The new resolution will be applicable to forest lands as well as other government wastelands.
* The development of forests will be done as per micro-plan and working plan provision will remain suspended for such areas.
* In earlier order village was the minimum unit for constituting VFPMCs but now even small hamlets can be unit of VFPMC.
* One member of voluntary agency or NGO can be in executive committee besides one member of Panchayat and concerned forester. All three will have no voting rights.
* General body of VFPMC will meet minimum two times in a year whereas executive committee will meet four times in a year.
* VFPMC can open account in any bank or post office and it will be operated with joint signature of chairman, member secretary and treasurer.
* VFPMC can impose pecuniary punishment on those who cause damage to forests. Similarly, VFPMC can levy charges for collection of NTFPs from their forests other than Tendu leaves and gums.
* In previous order final revenue was considered as net revenue which was to be shared whereas now gross revenue will be shared. When final felling will be made wood having less than 20 cm girth will be distributed free of cost to VFPMC members. But bamboo as well as wood with girth more than 20 cm would be sold by open auction. The sale proceed would be distributed in 3 ways:

    — Where the VFPMC has helped in protection only 80 per cent will be kept with FD and 20 per cent will be the entitlement of VFPMC.

    — Where VFPMC has rendered protection besides raising plantation out of their own resources—FD will be entitled for 10 per cent and rest 90 per cent will be retained by VFPMC but VFPMC will have to reinvest for future plantation out of its shares.

    — Where plantation is raised by FD and VFPMC has only rendered protection revenue will be shared on a 50:50 basis between them but for future VFPMC shall have to reinvest half of its share to raise plantation.

* Penal provision has been made in new resolution.
* Indication has been made how to resolve conflicts between various stake holders.

Thus new resolution is a step further in facilitating Joint Forest Management (JFM) on government lands as well as on forest land. In earlier order VFPMCs were not entitled for revenue from bamboo or "Munja" grasses whereas VFPMCs have been given right on these products in the new resolution.

Entry Point Activities

Realising importance of entry point activities which helps in developing trust between FD and the villagers, in welfare activities other than forestry activities, 15 per cent of forestry outlay has now been set apart for carrying out such development activities. These activities include construction of approach roads, water harvesting structures, community meeting place, hand-pumps, sheds for travellers and other skill development activities. Besides, executing agencies are directed to tap other rural development resources available with respective DRDAs for taking up development works in such villages. Since villages in the fringe of forest areas are located in remote corners usually development agencies other than FD do not reach such areas. Government of India has decided as a policy to transfer funds directly to FD as 100 per cent central assistance in all Integrated Afforestation and Eco-development Programme (IAEP) to take up different types of welfare works along with forestry. These works will be taken on pilot scale in few districts by forming Forest Development Agency (FDA). Such steps will certainly help villagers to develop forests under JFM and at the same time augment their community resources. However, such funds should be utilised judiciously otherwise the primary purpose of forestry development will be counterproductive. FD should take up these activities with full commitment and facilitate to strengthen the institution of VFPMC in a way such that sustainability of people's participation can be ensured over time.

Conclusion

Joint Forest Management (JFM) is only one of the several options available for forest management. If the forest management is not sustainable, sustainability of JFM is out of question. Hence, a meticulous planning is needed for the forest based on our understanding of both the ecological perspective and socio-economic imperatives. Indian society itself is now under an evolving phase in the face of many new trends like gender-equity, urbanisation, globalisation, consumerism, etc. Keeping in view these trends, the process of participatory approaches needs to be reviewed from time to time. A clear understanding of the problem, repeated consultations with the local people, sensitizing all stake holders and enhancing the institutional capacity will be required for the success of JFM. Since foresters have accepted such a challenge, the ultimate goal is to be achieved and then only can they prove their new role as agents of change.

5

A PROFILE OF MARAON, A PERI-URBAN VILLAGE IN VARANASI

SUDIPTA RAY

Introduction

Maraon is a village in Kashi Vidyapeeth Block of Varanasi District in Uttar Pradesh. It lies approximately 4.8 kilometres North-East to the Banaras Hindu University. Its shares border with Nakain village in its South, Dafarpur village in its East, Faridpur and Hasanpur villages in its South-East, Jafrabad village in its North-East, Hariharpur village in its North, Bhulanpur and Nathupur village in its North-West, Jalalipatti colony in its West and Pahari village in its South-West. This village was selected for the purpose of studying the significance of agriculture as a means of livelihood in a peri-urban village. This was done through participatory interactions.

The village is situated near the Diesel Locomotive Works (DLW) Colony which is 1.8 kilometres North-East to the village. As per scientific evidence the site has high level of sulphur dioxide and nitrogen dioxide pollutants. A government agriculture farm (Chandpur Village) is 2.52 kilometres North-East to the village. This site has high concentration levels of ozone, Sulphur dioxide, and Nitrogen Oxide.

The village being close to the DLW colony showed some urban characteristics. At the same time it had retained some of its rural flavour conditioned more by the circumstances like no proper approach road, lack of government initiative in setting-up education system and improper medical facilities, etc.

METHODOLOGY

1. Approaching Local Community

At the periphery of the village there was a middle school. One of the teachers in that school Shri Shankar Patel, was approached. After exchanging formal introduction and stating the purpose of the visit, it was learnt that he was also the Block Development Council (BDC) member of the village. Through his help some baseline data about the village was collected and later cross-checked with another group. Three other villagers Shri Patti Ram, Shri Dilip and Shri Bharat Lal joined in. The briefing about the village helped in selecting the wards for the purpose of the study.

Both the men and the women groups were interacted with separately. The age group ranged from 15 to 80 years. The groups did the following analysis: Seasonality analysis, Historical Analysis, Agricultural Constraints scoring, Field Observations, Cost-Benefit analysis.

Discussion Sites

In the absence of any other institutions in the village, the school run by the BDC was chosen as one of the discussion sites. Since the BDC also belonged to the Patel Basti, this site was utilised for conducting discussions with the members of the Patel Basti. Two of the participants volunteered to draw a rough sketch of the village. We then went for a joint walk partly through the fields and partly through the village. In the process, we got to meet more people. On reaching Maurya Basti and Harijan Basti, respectively, time was sought from the residents so as to learn from them at their convenience about their lives and livelihood strategies. The field study was then conducted in accordance with the time allotted by the groups.

Village Maraon is pre-dominantly Hindu with the dominant caste being the Harijans. The village has been declared Ambedkar Gaon last year. It is a medium-sized village with the number of total households roughly at 250. Farming system is semi-modern depending upon the financial resources available with the cultivator, his/her experience with the modern system and his/her age. The women of the village do majority of the agricultural field work except for buying the seeds, fertilisers and pesticides.

There are around 17 brick-kilns in the neighbouring village Bhulanpur. Railway line passes through the Maraon village. Maraon is an interior village. At its periphery (Nathupur village border and Jalalipatti border) colonies and slums comprising of service class and labourers are sprawling. The residents of these colonies and slums are either illegally encroaching agricultural lands in Nathupur village and Jalalipatti or are buying out agricultural land. Majority of the residents there belong to the neighbouring states and districts.

Demographic Details

As per the villagers, the village has a total population of about 2,500 residing in about 250 households. Only 30 per cent of the population is literate with the female literacy at 10 per cent. Average family size in the village is 6. The population is spread in a total of 7 wards as given below:

Wards	*HHS*	*Population*	*% in Agriculture*	*Main Occupation*	*Dominant Caste*	*Dominant Class*
Harijan Basti	100	1,050	0.05	Labourer	Scheduled	Lower
Maurya Basti	25	120	100	Labourer*/ Business	Maurya	Middle
Patel Basti	70	600	100	Labourer	Patel/Kurmi	Middle
Yadav Basti	10	80	100	Milk business	Yadav	Middle
Bowli Basti	30	300	25	Service/DLW	Mixed	Upper/Middle
Dalgiria Basti	10	50	99	Agriculture	Patels	Upper/Middle
Brahmin Basti	5-7	40	100	Government/ Pvt. Service	Brahmin	Upper Middle

* Labourers were referred to any work like factory worker, temporary worker, helper, agricultural worker, school teacher etc. who don't own agricultural land and minimum income is Rs. 1,500 p.m.

During group discussions with the local community it was learnt that they perceive basically four kinds of economic groups, mainly:

Economic Groups	*Group Definition*	*Population*	*Annual Income (Rs.)*
Poorest of the poor	Above 4 kids, no land, working as daily wage earner	5%	4,000 p.a.
Poor	Around 3 kids, no land, working as skilled labourer on contract, basis, might or might not possess land	20%	10,000 p.a.
Middle Class	In-between the poor and the rich	75%	1-2 lakhs p.a.
Rich	More than half of the family members in service class and owns 4-6 acres of land	less than 1%	4-6 lakhs p.a

Given that the economic groups defined by the villagers mainly focussed around land holding, it was felt essential to know the land holding pattern in Maraon which was as follows:

Small farmers	less than 10 biswa	70%
Middle farmers	less than 4 bighas	1%
Big farmers	more than 4 bighas	1%
Landless		25%

For the last 7 years government has initiated land consolidation in the village.

Land utilisation in the village is:

Total Land	121.01 hectares
Barren Land and residential	38 acres
Ponds (around 3)	2 acres
Agricultural land	260 acres

Soil depth in the village is 5-7″ and the water level is at 80ft. 5 per cent of the cropping is one borrowed land (shared or rent basis). The soil is clay in nature.

Seventy-five per cent of the population are still engaged in agriculture. Livestock also plays an important role in the livelihood of the local community. Their total population is up to 500 which includes pigs, goats, buffaloes and hens. Goat's population is the maximum which is about 200.

2. Livelihood Strategies of the Maraon Residents

After organising the men and the women groups in all the wards and building rapport with them, discussion was initiated on livelihoods pursued by the village community. The men and women groups were separately approached depending upon the availability of the groups.

The Process

* The men and the women groups identified three main seasons summer, rains and winter.
* For each of the seasons the participants analysed their livelihood strategies and livelihood constraints. They also described the nature of agriculture done in each of the seasons and highlighted the agricultural constraints.

* The men group in Patel Basti wrote down their analysis on a chart paper with the help of colored pens. Women group in the Harijan Basti also wrote down their analysis and sometimes explained with the help of 'visuals' and symbols for the benefit of illiterate participants. The active participant ('writer') in all the three groups read out the written analysis after conclusion of every topic to help the illiterate participants cross-check the outputs.
* Some other groups did their analysis orally. Semi-structured interview method was used for them. Sometimes, the participants drew on the ground or went to the farm to explain through agricultural samples.

The Analysis

From the seasonality analysis done by the group the following points emerge.

Livelihood

(i) Agriculture was practised by 75 per cent of the population and 25 per cent of the population worked as labourers.

(ii) Around 500-600 people in the village were engaged in *Banarasee Saree* weaving. To make one *silk saree* it took an average of 10-12 days. The maximum return one got from *saree* was about Rs. 1,100 (against Rs. 60 about 30 years back) whereas in the market it sold for Rs. 25,000-30,000 (against Rs. 2,500-3,000—30 years back). Some 30-40 years ago only 10-12 people were engaged. Now in the absence of any other job opportunity this was one of the high income source. In winter there was more work due to the oncoming festivals and ceremonies. For the last 4-5 years the market was reported to be depressed due to the government policy of liberalising import of silk. The interest in *Banarasee saree* weaving had developed due to the proximity of the village to Lohta which was the centre for sale of *Banarasee Saree*.

(iii) 75 per cent of the men were engaged in gambling.

(iv) There were around 10-15 HH in the village who were engaged in carpet weaving.

Livestock

(v) Livestock was kept mainly to fulfil the need of milk. It was an extra source of income generally for the Yadavs, who kept buffaloes and cows. Others mainly kept goats for personal consumption of milk because it was cheap price and low maintenance cost. However, goat gave milk only once a day hence sometimes, the owners were forced to buy milk from the Yadavs (traditional milkmen) or from the milkmen of the neighbouring villages. Best goat breed according to Maurya Basti was Jamuna Pari which came for Rs. 3000. An average breed gave about 2.5 litres/day. He goats were also sold for meat.

(vi) No household was solely dependent on agriculture. Consequently, any minor loss in agriculture was met by other sources of income. The strategy however, was to maximise the income by engaging the field throughout the year. Vegetables were grown most of the time with cereals sown late in the season only for personal consumption.

(vii) The groups opined that in the next ten years they would still continue with agriculture. Agriculture according to them could be managed by women and hence required less devotion of time by men. Men during their spare time could occasionally oversee the operations and at the same time work outside. The groups however, expressed their fear regarding the possibility of the encroachment of their land in the next ten years due to rapid growth of nearby colonies.

(viii) There were differences of opinion regarding the kind of service that would be preferred in the next 10 years. Some viewed that a labourer's job was the best as he did not have any fixed timings and can maximise his earnings by working at different places. Others viewed that opening a business was the best as one could operate from home and also the sprawling colonies would provide growth opportunities. Yet others viewed that if there was a possibility of getting permanent jobs in the factories then that would be the best due to the retirement and other benefits.

Below a pie-diagram (Fig. 5.1) shows their primary sources of income:

Role of Women in Livelihood

(a) Around 40 per cent of women supplemented income by making beads and Rudraksha necklaces. One of the villager was a sub-

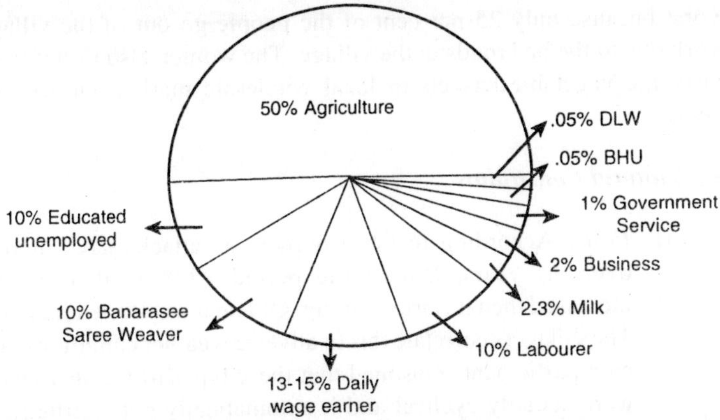

FIG. 5.1: The Primary Sources of Income

contractor of beads necklaces in the village. He generally bought back the necklaces. Other contractors from outside came and collected the necklaces or the women went to sell them. The necklaces were generally sold by the contractors in the remote villages of other states. Rudraksha necklaces generally got sold near the temples in Varanasi.

(b) Majority of the women were engaged in weeding of fields. They also carried the vegetables (if any) in a basket to the local wholesale market for sale. They also did sowing and tilling in the fields in absence of men.

(c) Ten per cent of the women made *bidis* (mainly women belonging to lower castes). Raw material was generally supplied by the contractor.

(d) Less than 5 per cent of the women worked as agricultural labourers during the season.

Lean Season

According to the groups, in the months of Chet and Baisakh the fields are empty (no vegetables) and hence there is no agricultural income. Vegetables cannot be sown during these months due to lack of proper irrigation facilities. Consequently, the cultivators are mostly free during these months. *Kuar* to *Phalgun* one receives income from agriculture. The month of *Aghan* is the best as income from vegetables especially cauliflower rises (the cost of cultivation is also the least and so is the expenditure on other sources). Rainy season was reported to be the worst because only 25 per cent of the people go out of the village to work due to the bad roads in the village. The women also find it risky to carry the vegetable baskets to local wholesale market due to muddy roads.

Agricultural Constraints

(a) *Pests:* According to the groups pests attacks have increased over the years. During the period 1988-91 their intensity increased then it started falling. Of late it has started increasing. The villagers correlate this to adverse weather conditions. Some men participants reasoned that these types of weather changes were actually cyclical and it automatically got rectified every third year (a leap year as per Hindu calendar and is referred as 'Malmas'). From 1988-91 the pest attack was so intense that majority of the cultivators reported that they discontinued growing cauliflowers in stretch for three years.

(b) *Natural:* Weather problems such as rain, hailstorm, frost and fog were rampant Rain during winter was considered to be harmful for the cauliflowers and also for the cultivators as they fell sick when compared with the monsoon rain.

(c) *Diseases* like hardwa and gurchawa were reported to be directly correlated to adverse weather conditions.

(d) *Lack of proper irrigation facilities* was identified as the biggest constraint in realising higher income in summer.

Maximum income from agriculture was realised in the winter season.

Till Phagun wheat was sown in the village. Cabbage was not grown that much in the village because moisture content of their soil was high and also its sowing time coincided with that of wheat. The cultivators usually made a choice between sowing spinach, raddish and cauliflower depending upon the resources like man-power, financial, resources, land size, proximity to land size, etc. available to them. Spinach was a low cost moderate return vegetable. Cauliflower was a high return moderate cost high labour vegetable.

The expenditure pattern in the village according to the groups is shown in Fig. 5.2.

Loans: Loan was generally taken by the villagers for agriculture, carpentary, ceremonies, opening shops, medical, and education purposes from fellow villagers or from the fertiliser shops in the town. Loan was also taken for gambling (among friends only) and alcohol (25% regular

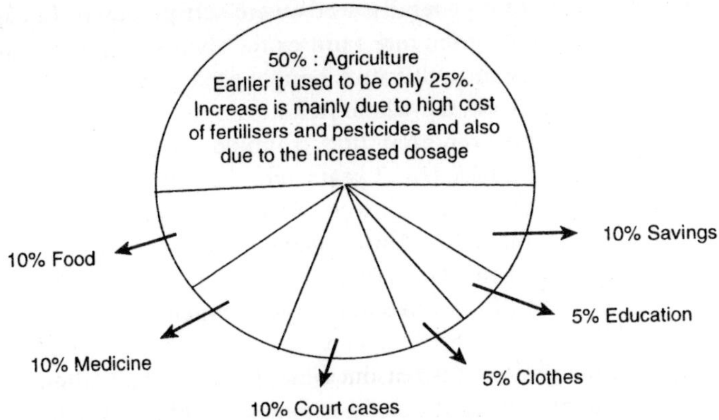

FIG. 5.2: Expenditure Pattern

drinkers). About 5 per cent of the population was under debt. Till 80's large agricultural loan used to be taken on 11 per cent rate of interest from the government agriculture farm or State Bank of India at Chandpur during the cauliflower season (Bhado-Kuar). Currently, also agricultural loan was taken in Bhado (loan up to Rs. 2,000-4,000) from fertiliser shops or village lenders (rate of interest 10% p.m.). To avail of large loans of Rs. 20,000 and above (very rare) they submited an application with the Kashi Vidyapeeth Block Development Office. Rate of interest charged on such loans was usually 12 to 14 per cent p.a. depending upon purpose. The loan was mainly given for installing pumpset, buying buffalo or tractor etc. Repayment had to be done within 2-3 years. In recent years loan was also taken from Dena Bank (Manduadih) for opening shops and Banarasee saree weaving centre. For large loans, the Gram Vikas Adhikary representative visited the borrower and inspected his assets and credibility before passing the application to the Dena Bank.

Experimentation: Endeavour of the cultivators in the village was to incorporate indigenous knowledge with modern farming techniques. Their information source was generally the programme on agriculture 'Krishi Darshan' shown on the television in Doordarshan Channel 1. Village visits by experts were also popular in the village. For example, the villagers very distinctly remember the farming techniques suggested by the students of Indian Institute of Pest Management, Kanpur who had visited the village in October, 1987. The villagers reported that they occasionally experimented either due to compelling circumstances or impressed by some new information. It was also learnt that:

(i) In agriculture generally seeds were self-prepared. In case, the government agriculture farm or the shop suggested some new variety then the cultivators bought seeds. The new variety was usually sown in the whole field.

(ii) Men groups reported that troubled by the increased pest ('Pankhi') attack 10-12 years ago, they sprayed phenyl (home disinfectant) on cauliflowers. Some of the cultivators also tried spraying molasses. Unfortunately, none of the experiments were successful. The participants said that the pests were under control for 20-25 years due to government sponsored spray of DDT.

(iii) All the groups were of the view that the actual administration of the prescribed dose of pesticides would also kill the plants.

Crop Rotation

The groups reported that generally the fields were engaged throughout the year (except for summer months) due to the improved irrigation facilities, new variety of seeds, pressure on income due to inflation, small land size compared to big family size, etc. Cereals were grown in small amount for personal consumption only. Wheat was sown in the field where paddy was grown in the previous season.

The men groups reported that crop rotation used to be practised some 20-25 years ago when the land holding size was big. During those days land naturally used to remain empty (or fallow) for one or two season at a stretch due to poor irrigation facilities. Very few could actually afford to cultivate paddy due to the small land size.

Sunui (green manure) was cultivated by some for the purpose of rope making and also for fertilising the fields for the crop in the next season (generally a high nutrient absorbing crop or vegetable). In earlier times, sunui, pigeon-pea, horse-beans, pea and gram used to be sown consciously to fertilise the soil for the next season. For the last 20 to 30 years this practise had been dropped forced by the circumstances.

After getting a picture of the current livelihood status and its various aspects, the discussion with the groups was focussed on the scenario prevailing in the village 30 years back.

Changes in the Village

The Process

Some of the elderly participants in the groups during the discussion on livelihood in the village kept comparing the current scenario with that prevailing during their youth. A discussion was initiated on the historical changes in the village after the independence. The participants recollected some of the significant events in the village which helped in identifying the reference time period. These were then sequenced decade wise. In case of any missing period, the groups were made to recollect it. Some results are given below based on the historical analysis done by group, in Maurya Basti.

1. *The Analysis*

(a) *Cropping Pattern.* For the last 15 to 20 years cauliflower had become one of the major commercial crop in the village. Earlier only Kuari variety used to be sown. But now due to the introduction of new varieties it got sown throughout the year. The other major crops were raddish and spinach (moderate income low cost vegetable). Extensive cultivation of vegetables was due to small land size involved in court cases (after the implementation of land consolidation by the government), improved irrigation facilities and nearby wholesale market. Only short duration and high income crops were preferred. In winter, cropping was done twice. Early in the season vegetables were sown (mainly cauliflower). Potato was sown by 5 per cent. Late in the season wheat was sown (only for personal consumption). Mustard was also sown with wheat for personal use only.

(b) 30 years back during summer—sugarcane, *kohra* and gourd used to be sown. 95 per cent of the land used to be fallow. During rain *Barsati Kohra, Ninwa, Sunui, Sawa* and *Jowar* used to be sown. 60 per cent of the land used to be fallow due to flood. Earlier agriculture was not done on a commercial basis. Presently, almost 95 per cent of the population sold their produce. Wheat and paddy were sold only by 2-3 households in the village who realised some surplus due to their large land size.

2. *Agricultural Constraints and Related Issues*

(a) According to the groups pest attack had taken serious proportion during 1989-91. The group in Patel Basti and Maurya Basti reported that the villagers got so desparate that they experimented by trying home disinfectant (popularly 'Phenyl'). Others tried molasses, but it also did not help. According to the groups the situation was so bad that some of the villagers stopped cultivating cauliflowers for the following two-three years. The pest attack was said to have dropped after 1991. But now again for the last 2 years it had increased.

(b) The womens of Maurya and Patel Basti reported that till 15 years ago they were spreading ashes on brinjals, lady's finger, etc. But had to look for other alternatives like pesticides when ashes started proving ineffective against pest attack. They however, still continued to spread ash whenever possible, it detered stray cows from grazing on the fields.

(c) Earlier due to lack of proper irrigation facilities 80 per cent of the fields used to be fallow during summer. Currently, only 40 per cent of the land remained fallow during the season, though for the same reason.

(d) Due to extensive cultivation of vegetables especially cauliflower pest attack had intensified. Application of pesticides had resulted in their resistance, hence frequent spraying was required. Generally powder was spread when the plants were small and spraying was done at a later stage. Every 10-15 days pesticides was given irrespective of any pest attack. The dosage of the pesticide was totally judgmental.

3. *Farming System*

(a) According to the group in Patel Basti natural manure like *dhencha, sunui* and *moong* apart from cow dung were good fertilisers and were used earlier. But presently cow dung was used more for fuel purpose due to non-availability of wood. Green manure crops were no longer grown because of small land size (and no commercial value).

(b) Due to improved irrigation facilities and new seeds extensive cropping of wheat started from 70's replacing barley and maize. Pumpset (first irrigation facility) was installed in 1976.

(c) Earlier ploughing used to be done by ox.

(d) The first fertiliser to be introduced was Chanmarkha in the late 60's which according to the men group in Patel Basti was one of the best. Current fertilisers were much inferior.

(e) Earlier crops were grown on the basis of soil quality. Like sandy soil was good for paddy. Nowadays it was decided more by the proximity to the irrigation facilities, land size and man-power availability.

(f) 40 years back gram, maize and pea were the main crops. Wheat was not sown that much due to irrigation problems. *Sawa* used to be sown instead of paddy. After the introduction of new paddy variety by government 20 years back paddy also became popular. Before that *Satthi Kakhhani* a variety of paddy (country variety) was used.

(g) Due to the introduction of new seeds and improved varieties atleast 60 per cent increase was reported in the population selling their produce (mainly vegetables). Wheat and paddy was sold by only 2-3 households. They were also the ones who employed agriculture labourers (women) @ Rs. 50 per day.

(h) Before the introduction of new wheat variety only 5-7 maund/ Bigha was available. Now, one got about 15-20 maund. However, with the increase in yield family size also increased and so also the division of land (due to break down of joint family system). Consequently, very few could afford to sell wheat and paddy after keeping aside for personal consumption.

4. *Standard of Living*

(a) 30 years back one used to have meal once a day especially during rainy and summer season. Poor people (belonging to lower caste) used to survive on *Mahua* flowers and fruits available from the village.

(b) During rain it was very difficult to go out because of water clogging.

(c) Earlier very few people were interested in agriculture as a source of income due to lack of facilities and damage done by the wild animals.

(d) To earn more people used to go to town and work as labourer. There was always some labour job available in the city due to Varanasi being a tourist spot.

During the historical analysis, the growing importance of agriculture in the village was felt. It was learnt that though the percentage of population engaged in it had fallen in absolute terms, in the relative terms it was now practised by the actual cultivators. In the back drop of this development, an analysis of the agricultural constraints and its future was done by the groups.

Agricultural Constraints in the Village

The Process

Men group (Patel Basti) and Women Group (Maurya Basti) had identified a list of constraints which they wrote down on a chart paper. Generally, symbols were used by the women group to represent the samples for the benefit of the illiterate participants. Detailed discussion was held on each of the listed constraints with the respective groups. The groups then prioritised the listed constraints with the help of stones for scoring which was fixed out of a score of 10.

The Analysis

1. Easterly winds were very harmful (mainly during monsoon months). This made the crops aphid prone. Crops affected were mustard, brinjal, *sem*, lady's finger and cabbage.
2. The pest attacks had increased in 1989-91. Then it fell. And now again for the last two years the pest attack has increased. According to few participants in the men group of Maurya Basti this was due to the adverse changes in the weather which takes place routinely and got rectified every third year (leap year in the Hindu lunar calendar).
3. Weather changes were mentioned by all the groups as one of the serious future constraints.
4. One of the reasons forwarded by the women group (Maurya Basti) for increased pest attack was spiders who's eggs gave birth to caterpillars (pest). The men group in Patel Basti reasoned that the faces of the moths (*Pankhi*) gave birth to caterpillars (*Jhansi*).
5. Extensive cultivation of vegetables especially cauliflower was considered to be one of the reasons for increased pest attacks. The main pests were *tel chatta, hara kira* and *jhansi.*
6. Few women participants in the Maurya Basti reported that due to the usage of pesticides, pest population get checked and hence it was not a major constraint. However, this had raised their expenditure on pesticides. Majority felt it was due to high cost of the pesticides. Few felt it was due to its increased usage. Some claimed that the poor quality of the pesticides and increased pests and their immunity were the factors behind

increased dosage. For all the groups stray cows and high cost of cultivation were the major constraints.

7. Excess rain in previous year (September beginning) damaged most of the cauliflower nursery.
8. Lack of proper irrigation facilities was one of the major constraints in summer due to which commercial cultivation of vegetables got restricted.

Field Observations

To understand better the agricultural constraints, fields were visited jointly with the groups. The groups showed the acute chlorosis of cauliflower leaves in the fields (south-end). The concerned cultivators reported this to be a new development this year. They also reported that the cauliflowers were deformed in the affected crops. *Jhulsa* disease was observed in onion in the fields. Incidence of damage due to *hara kira* was felt to be more in the south-end fields. In the eastern fields damage due to *Jhansi* was more.

During the agricultural constraints analysis it was learnt that smoke from the nearby chimneys was thought to be adversely affecting life in the village. Consequently, cost and benefit analysis was done by the group due to their proximity to the urban centre/industry.

Impact of Industrial Area on Maraon People

The groups orally analysed their perceptions of cost-benefit due to their proximity to industrial area. This analysis was done solely by semi-structured interview.

All the groups felt that the *benefits* due to their proximity to urban centre and hence industrial estate were as follows:

(a) A ready market for their vegetables where even the women could walk down every evening to sell their produce.
(b) Easy availability of labour work in the city.

The costs as perceived by the groups were however more than the benefits:

(a) Stray cows from nearby slums came and damaged their crops.
(b) Some water and air polluting industries were identified by the group like the brick-kilns, tyre companies, beads manufacturing companies, machine companies, cement companies, railways,

saree printing companies, indigo companies. The pollution from these factories was deteriorating air and water quality and was changing the climate. Pollution was also reported from increased vehicles and explosion of nuclear bombs and increased use of pesticides and fertilisers. Increased population and rapid expansion of urban centre was sited as one of the reason behind increased pollution.

4. Some of them mentioned that rapid urbanisation had given rise to a lot of brick-kilns in the neighbouring villages especially Bhulanpur. The fumes from these kilns, they felt, adversely affected their health, livestocks and crops.

Health

* Health was deteriorating due to poor food intake and crops using chemical fertilisers.
* Cold, cough and constipation had increased 4 fold in the last 10 years.
* Cases of tuberculosis had increased.
* In Asar the visit to doctor was more as per the women group (Maurya Basti).

Livestock

The participants in the group felt that due to slight deterioration in the air quality there was some impact on their livestock. During the discussion with the men group in Patel Basti one milkman from Jalalipatti joined in. According to him there had been an increase in the incidence of *Khangwa* disease among the buffaloes. Earlier it used to be only in Asar but now it took place throughout the year. This was happening for the last 1-2 years. Some of the participants added that this happened more when buffaloes were allowed to roam freely.

Crops

All the groups felt that there was some impact on the crops due to the poor air quality. According to them the smoke from the chimneys of brick-kilns and the other nearby factories:

* Lowered the mango yield due to burning. The mango size had also fallen in the last 10 years. Out of 100 trees only 75 trees fore fruits.

* Yellowing of wheat leaves were observed for the last 4-5 years. 75 per cent loss was reported due to this.
* One villager from Hariharpur joined the men group in Patel Basti. According to him, the wheat fields near the kilns showed small ear-rings. Marai people had not observed their wheat crops that carefully and asserted that the ear-rings were small in fields near the kilns. Since their fields were slightly far-off from the kilns they were not adversely affected.
* Some of the men participants reported that when train's steam engine used to pass through their village (5 years back), the fumes from the trains damaged the crops in the fields by the side of the railway track. There used to be black spots on cauliflower. They also reported that when the brick-kiln in the Marai village (operated from 1980-90) was in operation there used to be black deposits on the cauliflower. A farmer reported that he had incurred 50 per cent loss due to the fumes from the brick-kilns and steam engines.
* One farmer owning a mango orchard reported that due to the smoke from the brick-kilns in neighbouring areas, the mangoes tasted bitter. This happened because when mangoes were raw dust from the kilns fell on them. He had also observed black and yellow spots on the mangoes. Some of the mango trees now flowered less.
* Stippling of leaves has also been observed in Guava and Mango trees.
* Due to pollution crops had become weak and disease and pest prone.
* A brick-kiln was supposed to start operating from this summer. Men group gave a rough estimate of the loss due to this : 300 square yard of agricultural land would be acquired. In addition to that 20 yard land around the brick-kiln (in all the directions) would have to be kept barren. Crops will be damaged due to the smoke from the chimney because it will not be built at the prescribed height. There will be pollution of social environment due to settlement of outside labourers. Land will be mined up to 4-10 feet. Because of this rain water will clog there and might overflow into the neighbouring fields. Dust from the brick-kilns might damage the crops. Due to all this consequently, others will be forced to sell their land.

After the group had done cost-benefit analysis they identified their relationship with the the supporting institutions.

Institutional Set-Up

The villagers presented their relationship with the neighbouring institutions with the help of box diagram (explained to them by the facilitator) drawn on a chart paper as given below:

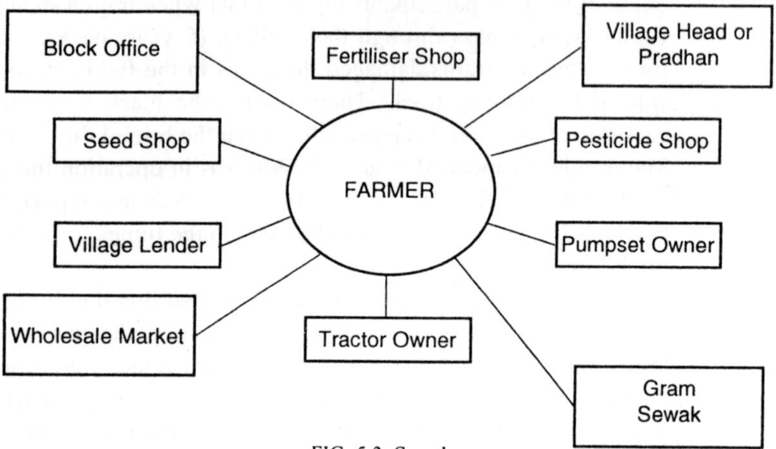

FIG. 5.3. Sewak

Village Analysts: Raj Narain Patel, Dudh Nath Singh, Shankar Patel, Kuar Patel, Ajay Pratap Singh, Dinesh Kumar Verma, Pratap Narain, Lallu Ram, Rajesh Kumar, Sesh Mani, Rajendra Prasad.

Facilitator: Sudipta Ray *Date:* 26.1.1999

Note: The participants first identified all the institutions with whom they come in contact regarding agriculture. With the help of the facilitator they represented each of the institutions with the help of a box with the farmer in a circle in the middle. Size of the box (in the ascending order) implied the relative importance of the institutions (in the increasing order). The distance of the box from the farmer indicated the closeness of the relationship shared by the farmer with the concerned institution.

On the basis of the above diagram, it was learnt that the:

(a) Seeds shop, fertiliser shop, pesticide shop, pumpset owner, tractor owner, village lender were of equal importance for the farmers. Wholesale market was drawn in a bigger box to show its high importance in their lives. This was due to the realisation of income from it. Village head, Gram Sewak and Block Office were drawn in slightly large boxes.

(b) The villagers did not share a close relationship with the village head, Gram Sewak and Block Office. With the Gram Sewak they were least close. Block Office was still closer.

(c) The villagers did not perceive any change in their relationship with the various institutions in the next 10 years.

(d) The group reported that the pace at which urbanisation was expanding, in the next ten years there would not be any land left in their village for agriculture and they will be forced to either work as labourer/open a shop or buy land in an interior village.

Field Results

From various analysis done by the village groups presented earlier one can deduce the following points.

(a) Vegetable cultivation was on a commercial basis in the village for the last 20 years. Among the vegetables cauliflower was the main.

(b) Small land sizes in the last two decades had resulted in a shift in the cropping pattern from cereals to vegetables (shorter cultivation time and high return). This had also been conditioned by the proximity to local market and improved irrigation facilities.

(c) Coarse cereals were replaced by wheat and paddy (mainly for personal consumption).

(d) Court cases due to government's recent imposition of land consolidation legislation in the village had lowered the area under cultivation.

(e) Smoke from brick-kiln (now closed) in the Marai village (5-6 years ago) used to damage the vegetables in the fields (5 years) and also resulted in black deposits on cauliflower.

(f) Fruit like mango was reported to have been adversely affected (75% loss) due to the smoke from the brick-kilns in the neighbouring areas. The size had fallen, the taste had become bitter and black/yellow spots were seen on the mangoes.

(g) The dose of fertiliser per *bigha* had increased in the last 25 years from that of 1 kg. to 5-10 kg.

(h) Pest (moths) attack had increased since 1985. It climbed to a peak in 1989-91. The problem became so serious that some of the villagers stopped growing cauliflower for following 3-4 years. While others in their desperation experimented with spraying Phenyl (home disinfectant) and molasses but failed. The pest attack after 1991 declined. Again for the last 2 years it showed an increase.

(i) Adverse weather according to some participants was responsible for increased pest attacks.

(j) Ashes used to be effective pesticide and fertiliser for Brinjal, spinach, and other leafy vegetables till 10-15 years back. But now it was increasingly proving ineffective. Consequently, the cultivators were forced to use pesticides.

(k) Due to fertilisers the weeds were also growing stronger.

(l) Bone potash (fertiliser) which was used some 20-25 years back was better than the current fertiliser.

(m) Pesticides usage had increased due to pest attacks, though no new pest variety had been observed. Extensive cultivation of vegetables had also been cited as one of the possible reasons.

(n) Interest in agriculture had increased over the last 30 years due to improved farming system. There had been increase of 60 per cent in the population selling their produce (mainly vegetables).

(o) Land utilisation was maximum in winter. In summer and rainy season lack of irrigation facilities acted as a constraint.

(p) For the last 2 years cauliflower was taking 120 days instead of 90 days to flower due to adverse weather conditions.

(q) Earlier only Kuari variety of cauliflower could be sown but now it could be cultivated throughout the year.

(r) Raddish and spinach were also grown throughout the year.

(s) Pollution was identified due to factories, brick-kilns, explosion of bombs, increased population, pesticides and fertilisers.

(t) Double cropping was done in winters to maximise income with vegetables sown earlier for sale and wheat sown later for personal consumption.

(u) Availability of poor quality pesticides forced the cultivator to increase the dosage. The pests were also becoming immune and hence again more quantity was required for effectiveness.

(v) Banarasee Saree weaving was one of the preferred occupation given one of the family member was engaged in agriculture. However, for the last 2-3 years it was not that high paying due to government policies.

(w) *Banjha* (sterility) was reported in pigeon-pea and brinjal crops.

(x) Future threat of agricultural fields turning into residential complexes due to rapid urbanisation was perceived by the villagers.

(y) Any loss in agriculture was generally met by savings from other income sources.

(z) Preference for agriculture as a complementary source of income would remain since the women could handle it independently.

(aa) Beads necklace making was becoming a popular income generation source for the women.

(ab) The villagers did not see any improvement in the relationship with the government support systems in the near future.

Selected Observations

(a) Women of the village did more than half of the field work. Men only ploughed the fields with the help of tractor or ox and bought the seeds, fertilisers and the pesticides. The men took the produce to the wholesale market on bicycle only if there was a huge surplus. Generally the seeds sown by the cultivators were bought 7-8 years back. The farmers made their own seeds. Hence, some of them failed to recollect the seed variety. Cauliflower seeds were bought generally by the farmers by the name of the month, like *Kuari, Phusi.*

(b) There was no support system like adult education centre, government schools, health centre, etc.

(c) Weeding in the grown vegetable fields was generally done every day.

(d) Commercial vegetables like cauliflowers and raddish were grown almost throughout the year.

6

PRA WORKSHOP ON BIODIVERSITY MONITORING WITH LOCAL COMMUNITIES OF MEHLI IN HIMACHAL PRADESH

VIRINDER SHARMA

Background

Sustainable Development requires the following:

A People Centred Approach, An Integrated Approach, Appropriate Technology and Institutionalisation to focus on the people's perspective, people's needs and also people's management. This is possible only through *people's participation*. Therefore, sustainable development has to be participatory development, and PRA facilitates participatory development. Participation is a process that enables people to express themselves, share, contribute, and act with mutual responsibility to promote a mutual set of interests. In the context of rural development, participation must consciously aim at promoting equity and sustainability. PRA starts the process of equitable and sustainable development.

PRA is a semi-structured and relatively quick way of learning with the rural people, about their situations, problems and opportunities. This way of learning requires the cultivation of certain attributes crucial to support people's participation, innovation, opinions and aspirations.

The objective of PRA is to arrive at an agreed set of possibilities for development, which could further lead to joint participation and mutual support in implementation, monitoring and evaluation. PRA can be described as a family of approaches, methods and behaviours that enable people to express and analyse the realities of their lives and conditions, to plan themselves what action to take, and to monitor and evaluate the results. Its methods have evolved from Rapid Rural Appraisal (RRA). The difference is that PRA emphasises processes which empower local people, whereas RRA is mainly seen as a means for outsiders to gather information.

The development professionals have better knowledge of modern science, new technology, the outside world and external resources, while the rural people are better equipped in traditional sciences, indigenous technology, local problems and opportunities and local resources. We have to learn from each other and thus act as partners in planning for development and PRA aims at this. The present note describes a PRA workshop of local community at Mehli on biodiversity monitoring.

Mehli site was selected for the training and capacity building of village communities for monitoring and conservation of biodiversity in Himachal Pradesh under the Indian-Australian Training and Capacity Building Project (IATCBP). The basis of selection were:

1. Biodiversity rich area
2. Presence of oak forest, grasslands
3. Availability of streamlets
4. Agriculture dominance
5. Presence of traditional houses as well as up coming of modern constructions.
6. Increasing pressure of urbanization which would threaten or disturb the ecology of the area in the near future.

Objectives

After the identification of Mehli as a site it was decided that baseline semi-quantitative information will be collected on the land use patterns, biodiversity, etc. through village level community registers and Participatory Rural Appraisal Methodology. The specific quantitative information will be obtained from the agencies. Geographical Information System will be developed for this area. With the integration and assimilation of the data, information will be interpreted and biodiversity indicators and actions required for restoration will be identified.

With this identification a systematic community based monitoring strategy will be developed and training will be imparted to village communities for their capacity building for monitoring and conservation of biodiversity. During the visit to Mehli site it was found that people of them village are very much linked and familiar with their local biodiversity. Although the urbanisation effect can be seen in the area but most of them are still doing local methods for the biodiversity conservation. They have good quality livestock and the milk/fodder capacity of village is satisfactory and it is playing a vital role in village economy.

A baseline information on locality background, changes in patterns over past few years in surroundings was collected through village level community register.

PRA Workshop

Such baseline information needed to be further quantified and cross checked. It was decided that a workshop using Participatory Rural Appraisal Methodology will be organised. With collaboration of Pradhan, Gram Panchayat, Mehli and Headmaster, Government Middle School Mehli, a workshop was organised on 12th October 1999, in the premises of middle school Mehli. Around 30 villagers and 40 school children actively participated in this workshop.

A welcome address and introduction of project, its purpose, objective and need of the villagers participation/(active involvement) was briefed by the team of outsiders. Pradhan Gram Panchayat, Mehli was pleased with the selection of Mehli as a site for this project. The officer said that we have been facing some changes in the grasslands, tree varieties and we need scientists' participation to assess the cause of these problems which may be due to our inappropriate conservation methods or common dilemma. And for this we have to revive our traditional values of conservation with active community participation.

After this, one facilitator drew a rough sketch of land use pattern in Mehli, and showed the transect in the village, the forests, the grasslands and water springs as the Project team had observed during the visits. The villagers were asked to draw their water springs, grasslands, agricultural fields, houses, forests oak as well as pine trees. Every person in the workshop got involved in the mapping process and identified their fields and forests etc. With the appraisal of this map it was found that the water sources which were earlier thought to be only 2 or 3 in number were actually 6 in number and were easily identifiable in the area.

After the mapping exercise, the villagers were interacted upon grass fodder variety. They were shown, the various grass specimen collected during the earlier visits, the communities immediately named the grass, the area where they are found, whether good or bad for cattle etc. In this way all the varieties of grasses were noted down on a chart paper with their uses, area, etc. After this the villagers were asked to quantify their availability and do the quality assessment on the rate of 100 and 10 scale respectively.

The people reported that the existing grass variety was good, and earlier two varieties of grasses were introduced by the Mahila Mandals but they were not that useful for them. Conservation of grasslands and Oak forests was in practice as these were not used for grass cutting and open grazing for 4-5 years due to community participation. With an assessment that the information on grass fodder was completed the team moved on to fauna species that were found in the grasslands and forests. The people reported that there were mantis (*Bhagwan Ki Gai*), Ghomphocerus (*Thadha*), Crickets (*Tiddian*), Rats (*Chuhae*) which were small and big in size and found in grasslands as well as in fields and houses. Small rats are called *chunger* and were found in grasslands. Chemicals were used to control their numbers and predators such as cats were domesticated. Mongoose (*Nevale*), Parrot, Magpie, Treepie (*Karate*), Hare-wild Rabbits (*Fararu*), Doves (*Malavae*), Pigeons were found. The fauna variety was noted down but their perception regarding their goodness or badness was not detailed and documented.

A Project team member briefed the plans of the Project to the villagers. Villagers told about their problems such as water scarcity, etc. and it was assured that if some provisions can be made then this village could be established as a model village.

After this exercise, the varieties of fodder trees were noted down which are Oak (*Baan*), *Kariyal, Mohru, Kemu, Khadak, Beol*, etc. But the quality and quantity assessment could not be carried out and it was decided that more information will be collected in some other workshops. Organisers of the workshop thanked the participants for giving their precious time for this workshop as during this time of the year they are generally busy in cutting grass and other activities.

PRA Outputs

1. *Changing Patterns in Fauna-Increasing Trends:*

Jackal	Rabbit
Mag pie	Tree pie
Rat	Parrot
Leopard	Mosquitoes
Malaya (LN)	Potato eater insect
Spider	

2. *Decreasing Trends in Fauna:*

Kakkar	*Ghural*
Water insects	Flies

3. *Flora: Changing Patterns*

Weeds (Bushes) have increased in the area.
Ageratun—White colour flowers—a weed has increased which destroys the grass.

The following additional information on fauna was collected:

1. *Leopard:* The number of leopards is increasing. The rate of increase is moderate and this increase has been observed from past 10-15 years. They are seen more in rainy season and winters around the village. They live in ravines below hill side. The reason for the increase is deforestation and stoppage of hunting. The leopards kills the village cattle. To control their menace villagers reported to the Forest Department and they trap the leopards and take them to the zoo.

2. *Mosquitoes:* Mosquitoes are big in size with long leagues, and are increasing at a fast rate in rainy season and in humid places. The increase has been reported since past 2-4 years due to increase in waste matter on the slopes. They are causing fever. As a measure of control villagers use smoke to repel them.

3. *Rats:* Rats found in the area are grey coloured and are both big as well as small sized creature (house rat, bandicoot). The rate of increase is constant from the past years and are found throughout the year. They live in fields and eat crops in fields, grains stored in house and chemical poison have been used.

4. *Parrots (Local Name Shooya):* The number is constant but as the corn/maize crops grow earlier in this place parrots migrate from other places to this area. Parrots destroy the crops as well as fruits. To draw them away from fields noise has been made through drum beating etc.

Biodiversity Collections by School Children

School children collected various plants and insects from the surroundings and recorded their local names. The insects collected by them were named in local language and were photographed. They made a chart and pasted the plants with their names and made notes on their uses, which are shown in Table 6.1. Table 6.2 shows the grasses ranked by the village community.

TABLE 6.1: School Child Collected Plants and Insects Named in Local Language

	Name	*Place*	*Uses*
1.	*Fegu*	Open place/hill side	Used in injuries
2.	Leaf of a flower	Flower Pot	Fragrance
3.	*Heere* leaf	Forest	Eatable
4.	*Kashmal* leaf	Open place/hill side	Eatable
5.	*Palam* leaf	Garden	Eatable
6.	Sweet leaf	Open place	Eatable
7.	*Kainth*	Open place	Eatable
8.	*Dudalae* leaf	Forest	Used in burns
9.	*Sadabahar* leaf	School ground	Ever green
10.	*Geedu* leaf	Forest	Used in vegetables
11.	*Palak* leaf	Surroundings	Eatable
12.	*Paaje* leaf	Forest	Eatable
13.	Yellow rose—*Peela Gulab*	Surrounding	Ornamental
14.	Thorn leaf (*Katewala patta*)	Open place	Eatable after extracting the thorns
15.	*Dhania*	Open place	Eatable
16.	*Gainda*	Garden	Medicinal uses
17.	*Palak*	Open place	Cattle
18.	*Siyar* leaf	Open place	Eatable
19.	*Dhaine*	Open place	Eatable
20.	*Gaindae* flower	Open place	Decorative
21.	*Samjora*	Forest	Eatable
22.	*Jeevan*	Open place	Evergreen
23.	*Baajaes* flower	Open place	Decorative
24.	*Shana*	Open place	Cattle eat it
25.	*Lal Gulab* (Red rose)	Garden	Medicinal uses
26.	*Jubal* leaf	Bushes	

TABLE 6.2: Ranking of Grasses by the Village Community

S.No.	*Grass Name*	*Properties*	*Quality assessment*	*Quantity (availability)*	*Changing pattern*
(1)	(2)	(3)	(4)	(5)	(6)
1.	*Baareek Ghas* Grass	Good for milch cattle, good for storage, not found in rocky areas	10	6%	Constant
2.	*Dagaryosh* (Grass)	Good for cattle only when it is green. Cattle does not like it. Cannot be destroyed easily. Rate of growth is high	5	10%	1% annual increase
3.	*Mota Ghas* (Chamb)	Cattle eat it when it is green. Found on the boundaries of fields available in larger amount. Earlier used for making mats	5	8%	Constant

(Contd.)

TABLE 6.2 (*Contd.*)

(1)	(2)	(3)	(4)	(5)	(6)
4.	*Joob*	Used for grazing by cattle and religious purposes. Harmful for crops, good for cattle.	8	1%	Constant
5.	*Khodhaey ka shana*	Good for cattle found in lesser amount and mostly near the water sources.	4	0.5%	Constant
6.	*Firgane*	Found in fields hard in nature not good for cattle.	2	0.5%	Constant
7.	*Fulnu*	Found on boundaries of fields in rainy season, good storage capacity for winters.	3	1%	3% annual increase
8.	*Kawaine*	Found in maize fields in rainy season and good for yield of milk in cattle.	8	1.5%	Constant
9.	*Piplu*	Good for high yield in milch cattle and found in rains, in fields.	8	2%	Constant
10.	*Shelu*	Harmful for cattle, used only when it is not ripe and before flowering.	−10	3%	Constant
11.	*Khatta Maloru*	Harmful for crops, cattle, do not eat.	−10	1.5%	Constant
12.	*Shada/Shayra*	Good for cattle in rainy season, good yield of milk and cream.	8	1.5%	Constant
13.	*Drab*	Used for fodder and religious purposes found on the boundaries of fields	7	0.5%	Constant
14.	*Dhara Dhaira*	Found in rainy season used for cattle when no other grass is available.	3	1%	Constant
15.	Others				Constant

7

RURAL PROBLEM PRIORITISATION AND PRA

SUMITA DAWRA

Introduction

At any given point in time, there are a number of ongoing programmes trying to alleviate rural poverty. The Integrated Rural Development Project (IRDP), Prime Minister's Rozgar Yojana (PMRY), etc. aim at income generation through asset creation; the Jawahar Rozgar Yojana (JRY), Employment Assurance Scheme (EAS) aim at wage employment and development of rural infrastructure; Indira Awas Yojana (IAY) looks after housing needs; Public Distribution Scheme (PDS) looks after basic needs of the poor at subsidized rates. In addition, we have a great variety of schemes for individual Sanitary Latrines, House site *pattas*, Rural Water Supply, Development of Irrigation Potential, not to mention the huge Watershed programme.

Despite so much money, energy and innovation being pumped into the rural system, the situation is still not one of having satisfied all the needs of the masses. In fact, the Gram Sabhas during *Janmabhoomi* programme, continue to throw up newer challenges for administration every time. And, like Alice in Wonderland, one has to run faster and faster to be at the same place.

The present study indicates problems as prioritised by rural, poor women in the coastal, delta Krishna District of Andhra Pradesh. The data generated may be of use to policy-makers, NGOs, donor agencies in planning inputs to the rural system.

Goals of Study

Keeping the above in mind, and with a view to generate comprehensive and focussed information on the priority needs of the rural poor, an exercise was done in April, 1999, in rural areas of Krishna District, to

(i) identify the various problems the rural women experience, and
(ii) to prioritize these problems by ranking them.

Thus, as opposed to assessing total problems in rural areas, focus was kept on identification and ranking of problems as perceived by rural women who were Below Poverty Line (BPL).

Area of Study

The study was confined to the rural areas of Krishna District. Locations numbering 947 were covered by the study falling into 726 villages, of which 450 number of villages were upland and 276 number of villages fell in delta area of the Krishna river.

The Krishan district, itself, is a Coastal District of Andhra Pradesh, with an area of 8336.25 sq. kms., a population of almost 42 lakhs people, 26.95 lakhs of which are in rural areas. Out of the total 49 mandals, 21 number of mandals fall in the productive Krishna delta area, and 28 number of mandals are upland.

As per the most recent Below Poverty Line (BPL) survey conducted, 1,13,460 of families, *i.e.*, 21.05 per cent of total population of the rural areas, are below poverty line as defined by Rs. 216.65 per capita monthly consumption.

Methodology

The sample selected for the study were the women belonging to Development of Women and Children in Rural Areas (DWCRA) groups, Self-Help Groups and Mahila Mandals in the rural areas of Krishna district.

It was decided to use Participatory Rural Approach (PRA), in order to generate maximum participation of the target population and to do away with the planner's bias in leading the process.

Problem scoring method was used whereby the participants of the village, namely members of DWCRA groups, Mahila Mandals, were asked by the local Anganwadi Worker/Cluster Volunteer to generate problems faced by them. The problems were noted on the ground as they were generated. Once this process was exhausted, the women were encouraged to discuss and decide which was the problem, out of the many identified, which was felt by them as the most severe one and to place maximum number of Pebbles/Stones/Flower/Pulses, etc. under that problem. Then go on to the problem perceived as next most important and so on.

The ranking was accordingly noted down by the Coordinator of the PRA, exercise by giving rank 1 to the problem carrying maximum pebbles, rank 2 to the problem carrying next number of pebbles and, thus, a descending order of ranking of problems was obtained for the habitation/village.

In this fashion, 947 number of PRA exercises were done in 726 number of villages and a ranking of identified problems obtained.

For proper conduct of the study, 1631 rural *Anganwadi* workers and 365 Cluster Volunteers of DWCRA were trained in the method and its do's and don'ts, in 13 training camps, spread over a total of 6 days, between 1 to 11th April, 1999. For conduct of PRA, familiarity of the target population with the person conducting the study is most crucial. No one will speak freely to a stranger. Sometimes, it may be required for a new person to visit the area of study for long periods before that level of familiarity is achieved. This problem was, however, avoided since the Anganwadi Workers/Cluster Volunteers who conducted the study were normal residents of the area and interacted with the women on a daily basis, in the course of conducting their professional duties.

Data Analysis

The data received from 947 habitations/villages was computerized completely, habitation/villagewise, and the problems identified entered in descending order of ranking. Thereafter, computer programming was done to list out the problems identified and their frequency of identification entered, percentage-wise.

TABLE 7.1: Identification of Various Problems in Rural Areas

S.No.	*Problem*	*No. of times identified*	*Percentage of total*	*Percentage of locations in which identified*
(1)	(2)	(3)	(4)	(5)
1.	Latrines	947	13.75	100.00
2.	Ration cards	623	9.04	65.79
3.	House sites	584	8.48	61.67
4.	Drinking water	580	8.42	61.25
5.	Pensions	529	7.68	55.86
6.	Drainage	476	6.91	50.26
7.	Roads	444	6.45	46.88
8.	Electricity	347	5.04	36.64

(*Contd.*)

TABLE 7.1 (*Contd.*)

(1)	(2)	(3)	(4)	(5)
9.	Anganwadi centres	255	3.70	26.93
10.	Medical aid	222	3.22	23.44
11.	House construction	214	3.11	22.60
12.	Bus facility	207	3.01	21.86
13.	School/High School	188	2.73	19.85
14.	Boring pumps	159	2.31	16.79
15.	Veterinary Hospital	120	1.74	12.67
16.	Loans	92	1.34	9.71
17.	Street lights	73	1.06	7.71
18.	Library	71	1.03	7.50
19.	Benefits for physically handicapped	69	1.00	7.29
20.	Clean and green	68	0.99	7.18
21.	Community hall	59	0.86	6.23
22.	Ladies benefit funds	51	0.74	5.39
23.	Request for bus stop	47	0.68	4.96
24.	Sewing machine	47	0.68	4.96
25.	Literacy	32	0.46	3.38
26.	Self-employment	32	0.46	3.38
27.	Cyclone shelter	31	0.45	3.27
28.	Problem of stray dogs	29	0.42	3.06
29.	Child welfare centre	28	0.41	2.96
30.	Ration shop	26	0.38	2.75
31.	Smokeless furnaces	25	0.36	2.64
32.	Handicrafts	20	0.29	2.11
33.	Milk booth	19	0.28	2.01
34.	Burial ground	17	0.25	1.80
35.	Post box	16	0.23	1.69
36.	Request for Gram Panchayat Office	16	0.23	1.69
37.	Super gas	15	0.22	1.58
38.	Illicit liquor	14	0.20	1.48
39.	Formation of Self Help Groups (SHG)	12	0.17	1.27
40.	Telephone facility	12	0.17	1.27
41.	Side walls	12	0.17	1.27
42.	Maternity benefits	11	0.16	1.16
43.	Land for agriculture	9	0.13	0.95
44.	Removal of mosquitos	8	0.12	0.84
45.	Tank for washermen	5	0.07	0.53
46.	Wages	5	0.07	0.53
47.	Group insurance	4	0.06	0.42
48.	Vegetable market	4	0.06	0.42
49.	Price control	4	0.06	0.42
50.	Maternity doctor	3	0.04	0.32
51.	Protection from thieves	2	0.03	0.21
52.	Vocational education	2	0.03	0.21
53.	Bus shelter	2	0.03	0.21
54.	Weaving facility	1	0.01	0.11
	Total	6,888		

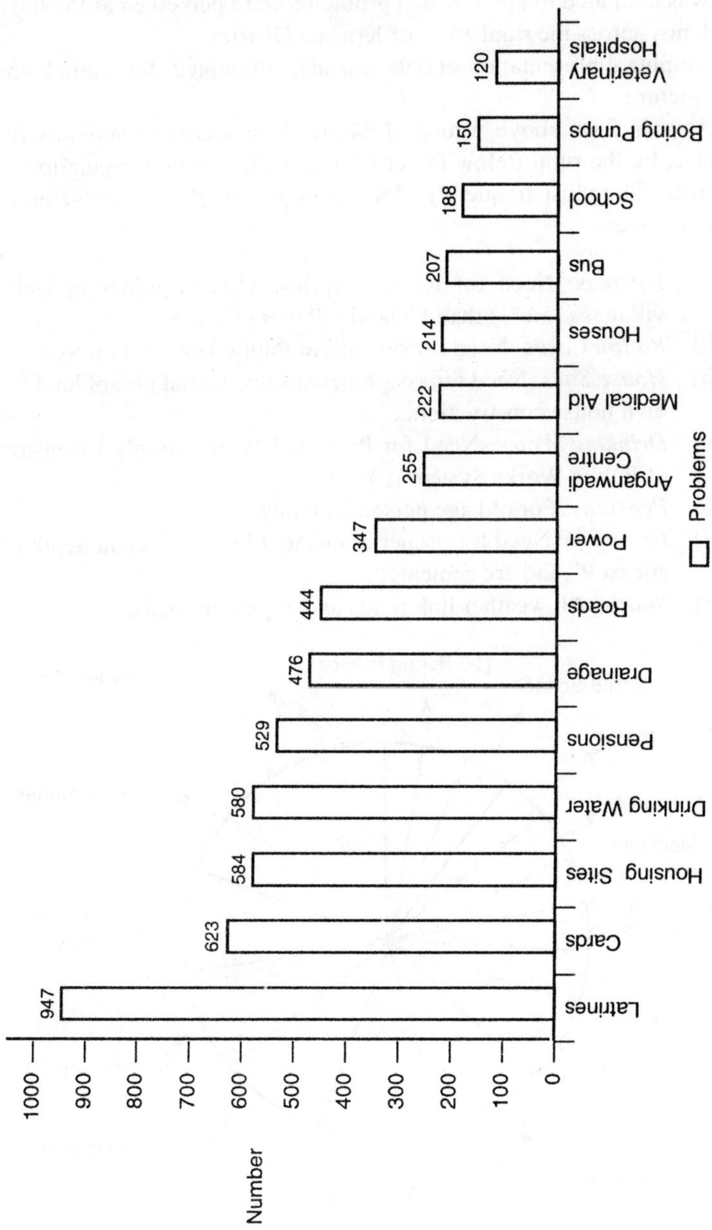

FIG. 7.1: Krishna District—Top 15 Rural Problems Generated

Subsequently, frequency of identification of a problem at rank 1, 2 or 3 was tabulated to know which problems were perceived as the top 3 problems, across the rural areas of Krishna District.

Graphical presentation of data was also attempted, for a quick and clear picture.

As seen from above, a total of 54 problems were generated by the exercise, by the rural Below Poverty Line (BPL) women population of the areas. The most frequently (5% and more) identified problems of these area were:

(i) *Latrines:* Need for toilet facilities; This is higher in Delta villages (15.6%) than Upland villages (12%).

(ii) *Ration Cards:* Need for subsidised Public Distribution System.

(iii) *House Sites:* Need for assignment of residential plot of land for own house construction.

(iv) *Drinking Water:* Need for Protected Water Supply/Extension of Public Works System (PWS).

(v) *Pensions:* For old age persons, mainly.

(vi) *Drainage:* Need for proper drains that have sufficient depth of atleast 9″ and are cemented.

(vii) *Roads:* All weather link roads and approach roads.

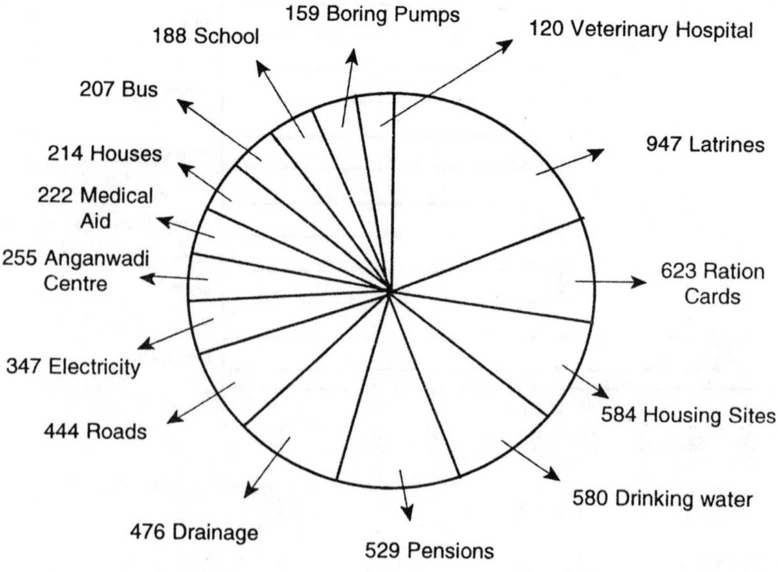

Fig. 7.2: Krishna District—Top 15 Rural Problems Generated most Frequently

(viii) *Electricity*

(ix) Also, in high demand are Anganwadi Centres, medical aid, house construction and bus facility.

TABLE 7.2: Frequency of Identification of Various Problems in Rural Areas as Top Rank Problems

Sl.No.	*Problem*	*Rank 1*	*Rank 2*	*Rank 3*	*Total*
(1)	(2)	(3)	(4)	(5)	(6)
1.	Latrines	259	233	187	679
2.	Drinking water	268	108	61	437
3.	House sties	135	104	84	323
4.	Ration cards	75	125	123	323
5.	Drainage	43	92	99	234
6.	Roads	73	78	75	226
7.	Current	39	51	66	156
8.	Pensions	23	38	67	128
9.	Bus facility	32	46	29	107
10.	Anganwadi Centres	28	32	39	99
11.	House construction	22	30	45	97
12.	Medical aid	36	33	24	93
13.	School/High School	25	21	26	72
14.	Boring pumps	26	15	24	65
15.	Veterinary Hospital	19	24	21	64
16.	Loans	6	15	15	36
17.	Library	7	8	16	31
18.	Street lights	3	14	13	30
19.	Community Hall	11	12	6	29
20.	Benefits for physically handicapped	6	10	6	22
21.	Clean and green	1	10	9	20
22.	Request for bus stop	3	9	7	19
23.	Sewing machine	7	8	3	18
24.	Cyclone shelter	1	7	9	17
25.	Ration shop	4	5	6	15
26.	Smokeless furnaces	0	1	8	9
27.	Handicrafts	1	2	5	8
28.	Stray dogs	1	5	2	8
29.	Ladies Benefit Fund	0	2	6	8
30.	Formation of Self-Help Group (SHG)	1	1	4	6
31.	Post box	1	1	4	6
32.	Illicit liquor	5	1	0	6
33.	Milk Booth	0	3	3	6
34.	Burial ground	3	1	1	5
35.	Request for Gram Panchayat Office	1	3	1	5
36.	Telephone facility	1	1	3	5
37.	Side walls	1	2	2	5

(*Contd.*)

TABLE 7.2 (*Contd.*)

(1)	(2)	(3)	(4)	(5)	(6)
38.	Literacy	2	0	2	4
39.	Self-Employment	0	3	1	4
40.	Removal of masquitos	2	0	1	3
41.	Maternity benefits	1	2	0	3
42.	Child Welfare Centre	2	0	0	2
43.	Maternity doctor	1	1	0	2
44.	Bus shelter	1	1	0	2
45.	Tank for washermen	0	0	1	1
46.	Weaving	0	0	1	1
47.	Vegetable market	0	0	1	1
48.	Price control	1	0	0	1
49.	Wages	0	1	0	1
	Total	1,177	1,159	1,106	3,442

Of the total 54 problems identified by rural BPL women, 49 problems received a rank of 1, 2 or 3. This shows that though only 8 problems occurred at a frequency of 5 per cent and more, as per Table 7.1, the less frequently reported problems were of an important nature in the villages where they were identified. For example: Ration shop was identified as a problem in only 26 places (Table 7.1), but it got rank 1 in 4 villages, rank 2 in 5 villages and rank 3 in 6 villages, making it a problem of paramount importance in atleast 15 places where PRA was conducted (Table 7.2).

Further, problems reported as problems of greatest magnitude (having obtained rank 1, 2, or 3)in maximum number of places (having obtained rank 1, 2 or 3 in more than 100 places) are:

		Overall Rank
(i)	Latrines	1
(ii)	Drinking water	2
(iii)	House sites	3
(iv)	Ration cards	4
(v)	Drainage	5
(vi)	Roads	6
(vii)	Electricity	7
(viii)	Pensions	8
(ix)	Bus facility	9

It is understandable to see rural BPL women identify latrines as their greatest need. The delta areas, where land is so expensive, where paddy fields cover every inch of land available, earmarking separate land for women's community toilets, is a luxury. The individual sanitary latrines offer an opportunity to the women to build toilets in their house at a subsidized rate. However, not everybody gets a sanction, with total no. of such sanctions in 1997-99 being 53,014 units with Rs. 1060.28 lakhs Govt. contribution, at Rs. 2000 each. That means, as such, about 53014 Below Poverty Line (BPL) families were sanctioned a sanitary latrine unit. Need for latrines emerged as a number 1 rank problem for both delta and upland mandals. Though, in delta villages, 15.6 per cent was the weightage (in terms of no. of times the problem was identified) received for the problem in total data of delta areas and 12 per cent was the weightage received by the problem in the total data of upland areas.

Secondly, even with no village in Krishna district having drinking water source outside 1.6 kms. radious, drinking water emerged as the second most important problem in rural areas (both upland and Delta), for the BPL women. One reason could be that there were only 571 no. of Public Works System (PWS) schemes in the district, with 63 per cent of revenue villages covered. This was possibly on account of the need for PWS, or if PWS was there, on account of distances involved in carrying the water to the house (there was often a demand for extension of pipelines for PWS scheme till the road on which they resided, or, even, till their doorstep).

In Delta areas, the high possibility of contamination of drinking water tanks from the extensive fish/prawn cultivation was another factor making drinking water a problem. Frequently, the outlet of the fish/prawn tank met the inlet to the Drinking Water Tank from the canal, thus contaminating the water. Sometimes on account of lack of fencing for the drinking water tank, the villagers perceived it as unsafe drinking water, despite the PWS filters, on account of high rate of open defecation in the vicinity of the source. In such cases, the villagers prefer bore wells as a drinking water source. However, a bore could not supply water for a large population in Black cotton soil or sandy coastal areas of Delta, since permeability or brackishness, respectively, was a constraint. In uplands, dependence was more on bores and the PWS were also built on deep bores and not on open tanks. Falling groundwater level or repairs to these bores during summer months, all contributed to drinking water being identified as a problem.

House sites, ration cards, drainage and road facilities were also very real problems. With lot of families living as tenants, addition of newly married population, need for house sites remained high, especially with each beneficiary in rural areas desiring an independent, single storey

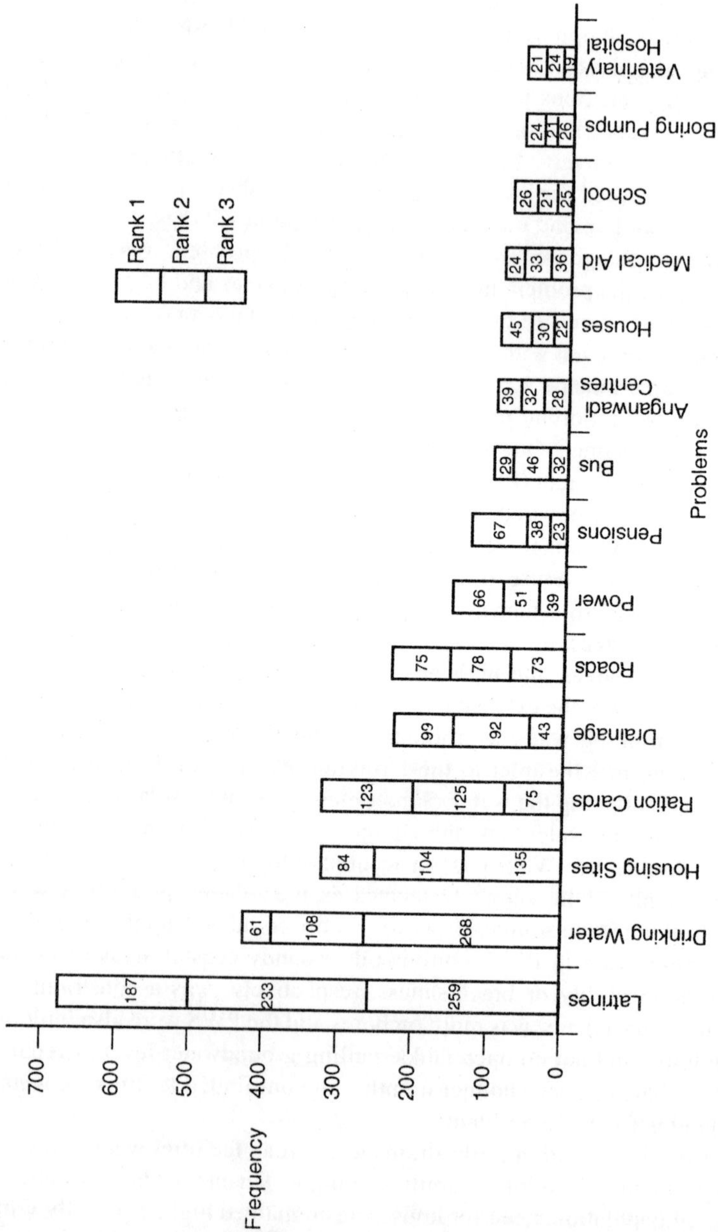

FIG. 7.3: Krishna District—Top 15 Rural Problems Generated most Frequently

dwelling unit. With respect to ration cards, the need was mostly for the white card that gave access to subsidized rice of 20 kg. per BPL family.

In Krishna district, 6.8 lakhs No. of families possessed a white card, yet the demand was high due to various factors such as high number of bogus cards, increasing number of newly formed families, etc.

Overall, lack of latrines was a more consistently identified important problem since it got all 3 ranks (rank 1, 2, 3), highest number of times.

However, it is to be noted (see stacked bar diagram, Fig. 7.3) that drinking water got identified as rank 1 problem maximum number of times, while latrines got identified as rank 2 and 3 problem maximum number of times. This indicates that in 268/947 (28.29%) of study locations, drinking water was the most severe (rank 1) problem. Also see Fig. 7.4.

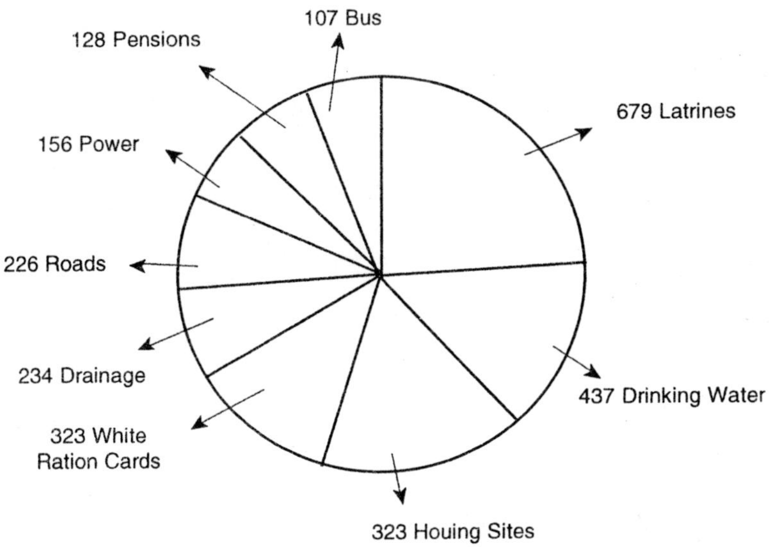

FIG. 7.4: Krishna District—Rural Problems of Greatest Magnitude

Some conclusions from the ranking exercises are as follows:

* Need for Latrines (Toilets), Ration Cards, House Sites, Drinking Water, Pensions, Drainage, Roads and electricity were *most frequently generated as problems* in PRA exercises with BPL families is rural areas in Krishna district.
* These 8 problems put together were identified as problems

65.77 per cent of times, emerging as the 8 most frequently prioritised problems of the rural areas in Krishna district.

* Of all the needs generated, need for toilets and drinking water were identified by rural women groups as *problems of greatest magnitude* (having attained ranks 1, 2 or 3 maximum number of times), in rural areas. Both put together, achieved Rank 1, 2 or 3, 32.42 per cent of times.
* Toilets, drinking water, house sites, ration cards, drainage and roads, put together, achieved ranks 1, 2 or 3, 64.56 per cent of times, emerging as the *6 most important problems* of the rural areas of Krishna District.

8

CHILDREN'S PERCEPTION ON LIVELIHOOD

BRATINDI JENA

Promotion of sustainable livelihood has become an important objective of development programmes. Both economic and social development programmes aim at providing secured living and meeting basic needs. However, often programmes and activities are forced on people without knowing their interest, environmental conditions and societal structure. Any activity that does not suit the area fails to last long. In todays situation it is important to understand the people of the area and all related factors to make any programme successful. Participatory Rural Appraisal gives people enough space and opportunities to express themselves and make others understand their situation and need.

PRA is intended to enable local people to conduct their own analysis and often to plan and take action. It means transforming the old depending roles and recognising local people, both men and women, as active analysts, planners and organizers (Chambers and Guijt, 1995).

One important issue in this context is that of children's views sustainable development programme needs to include views of the coming generation. Otherwise it might fail to sustain itself in the long run. In a fast changing world children lead a stressful life and are often the bread winner of family. It is they who have their problems and priorities and often do not have enough opportunities to discuss and resolve them. Therefore, it is essentials to have discussions with children for organizing any programme related to livelihood.

PRA with children helps in getting a clear expression of their feelings and emotions. By involving children in development planning and addressing their needs, emphasis, is on integrating child focused analysis and gender perspective with in the over all frame of analysis of any given society.

The utility of drawing as a PRA tool with children confirmed that creative activities are usually popular with them. It proved to be an important tool for initiating the research process as it was easy to implement and in overcome the barriers of illiteracy and muted silence (Sapkote and Sharma 1996).

This exercise of drawing gives children enough freedom to express them selves and understand and interpret the world around them in their own way. However, when we compare boys and girls the situation is considerably different.

Girls in almost all parts of India lead a low status with unequal opportunities and heavy burden of responsibility. In the desert area of Rajasthan this increases further. Girl children have to walk miles in the heat to collect fuel wood, fodder and fetch water. They graze livestock, gather wild grown fruits and vegetables. In the summer months it is difficult to move around for even an hour in that area. But children spend the whole day working under thin shade of a tree, here and there.

Sekhasar is a desert village in Tehsil Phalodi, district Jodhpur. This village is about 200 kilometer from Jodhpur and 130 km. from Bikaner. The nearest market and Panchayat Samiti is about 32 km. away and the tehsil is 25 km. The area in hectares is 11,41,864 and number of occupied residential houses are 358. total population of the village is 2,421, of which males are 1,270 and females are 1,151. Total population of the age group of 0-6 is 250.

This village is about 500 years old. It has the history of *jagir* system. Rajputs of this area were the first one to come and settle down here then they got people of other caste for their convenience. *Rajput Bhil, Beldar* (earth worker), *Meghwal, Delhi, Nai* and *Potter* are the different castes residing here. However, even after abolition of *jagir* system the village is dominated by *Rajput.*

There is only one source of drinking water both for human consumption and livestock. It has a government middle school. Children from five villages study in this school. There are no proper road linkages and poor commuting services.

Livelihood Pattern

In this area peoples' livelihood depends on land, labour and livestock. Land cultivation and crop productivity depends on pattern of rainfall. Livestock also depends on land for fodder as there is not much scope to get green fodder otherwise. This is the source of income generation with in the village. Families are settled in disperse settlement in mud huts next to their field, that help them guard their land and livestock. Land cultivation depends on rainfall because no irrigation facility is available. Soil is hard and sandy, cultivation by tractor has helped in better production. Livestock maintenance still remains to be an important source of income. They have livestock like sheep, goat, cow and camel. During post harvest seasons, people migrate as labourers to distant places like Punjab, Haryana and Gujarat. The nearest labour market is the salt mine of Rin (Bap) and stone quarry, women and children spend summer days either working in the nearest salt mine or collecting wild grown fruits and vegetables. Though never recognised, children spend a lot of time working with the parents either in the field, livestock rearing or in labour market and contribute to the livelihood pattern of the family. Those who do not work in any of these areas, they collect wild grown summer fruits for consumption the whole year.

Objectives

The main objective was to learn about children's understanding of livelihood. This exercise gave them a chance to express their views on sustainable livelihood. Drawings followed by discussions expressed their gender biased conditioning right from childhood. Faculty expressions in their role playing was quite evident.

Group of Children

This exercise was done with both boys and girls studying in the school. There were 6 boys and 5 girls. The age group was between 10 to 15 years. All of them were quite regular in their study. The group was small in order to facilitate proper discussion and give individual attention to their expression. Only those children willing to participate in this exercise were included in the group.

Process

This exercise was initiated because of the children's interest. In fact girls were more interested in these meetings.

In the local school there are 148 boys and 43 girls. Girls were not allowed to study after class V, except for one or two girls studying up to class VII. Rapport building was easy because all the children knew the facilitator well.

The first exercise was to draw pictures indicating ideas on secured livelihood which would secure their livelihood, help development of the coming generation and the village. This included drawings that would indicate their basic needs.

Drawing Exercise

This exercise was carried out inside a classroom of the school. There were chart papers and colour pens. Boys wanted to sit separately and do the work individually. They took more space and did not wish any one to see their drawings. Whereas, girls wanted to sit at close proximity so that they could work together, see what the others are drawing and all wanted to sit in a corner away from the boys. All were requested to sit separately and do this exercise.

In the beginning we started talking about different types of livelihood and means to strengthen them in a group. During our discussion, children expressed a clear vision of different types of work done by people in their village and the problems they faced. Through drawings they could express their thought more effectively. After they completed the work we started discussing about the drawings they had made.

Girls had drawn:

* School,
* rooms,
* weighing machine, and
* temple.

During our discussion, It was asked how would the school help in securing their livelihood. Their answer was clear that the people were not able to earn much in whatever work they do because they were illiterate. They do not get proper work and often get cheated. If they have a proper school and children start studying it will be a great thing for the future of the village. They had a long list of demands for the betterment of the existing school. More teachers, repairing of school building and appointment of a female teacher came as their first priority. Parents do not send girls to school after class V. Because there is no women teacher, children are not able to express their problems in front of the teachers, because they are all men. There is no toilet for girls, no library and games available. Teachers are irregular and do not teach properly.

A proper house was the next item. They all live in small mud huts. Get very little space for anything they want to do. No space to sit and read or start some kind of work. In fact girls have no space at home. When visitors or elderly people sit inside a room girls are expected to be outside.

TABLE 8.1: When asked about Secured Livelihood Girls mentioned these Factors and Scored them according to priority

Girls Priority	*Scores*	*Ranks*
School	10	1
Road	8	3
Weighing Machine	6	5
Temple	7	4
Proper House	5	6
Water Tank	9	2

A weighing machine is required to weigh every item before they sell to the merchant who visits the village. In this village merchants visiting from nearby town guess the weight of the sack and pay the price. This is done with agricultural products, wool and lamb. In this process they do not get the actual price for the product. Children have started realising the problem. Temple needs to be in good condition, so that they can go and worship. If everyone goes to the temple before starting their days' work they will remember to do good things, help each other and create a healthy social environment. Whereas now they fight over small matters and create disturbance and unhealthy environment in the village.

Boys gave importance to:

* Electricity supply,
* Tube-well,
* Bus (commute), and
* Hospital.

Since there was no irrigation facility available, crop failure is quite common in the absence of rainfall. Tube-well would help in irrigation of land and better yield. Electricity is needed to start any type of small repairing shop, mill, etc. In the absence of electricity children are not able to study. There is no proper commuting facility available to the villagers. This is one of the hurdles people face if they want to go and work outside. Often work is hampered because of this. One boy drew a hospital. There is no medical facility available in the village and nearest place is about 32 km. In the absence of proper transportation system people face a lot of problems.

Drawing by Girls

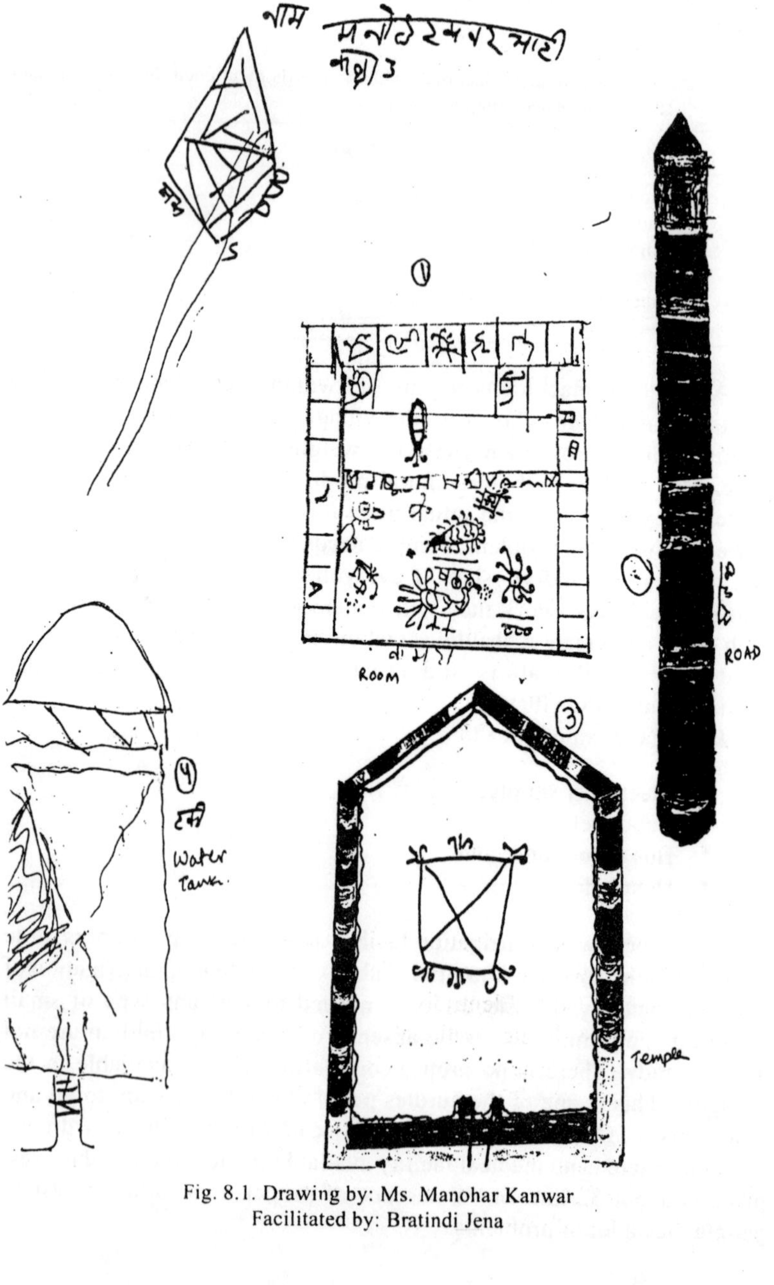

Fig. 8.1. Drawing by: Ms. Manohar Kanwar
Facilitated by: Bratindi Jena

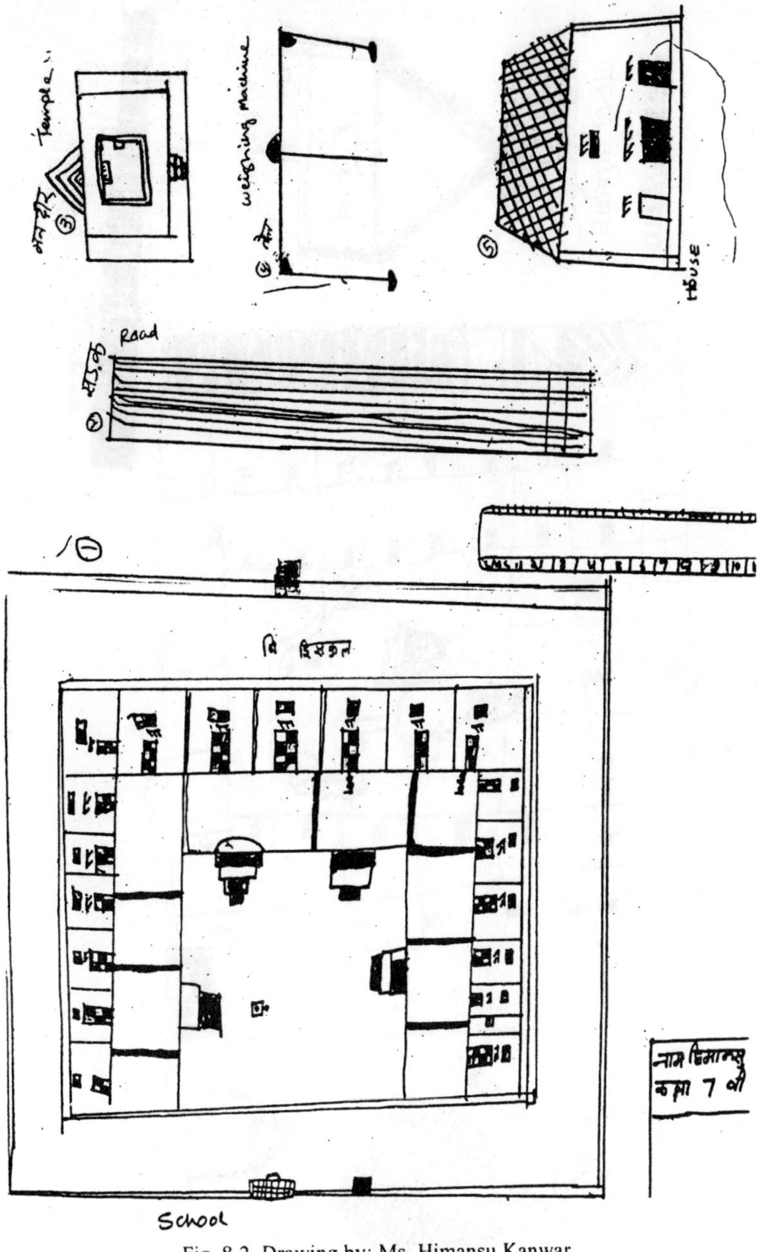

Fig. 8.2. Drawing by: Ms. Himansu Kanwar
Facilitated by: Bratindi Jena

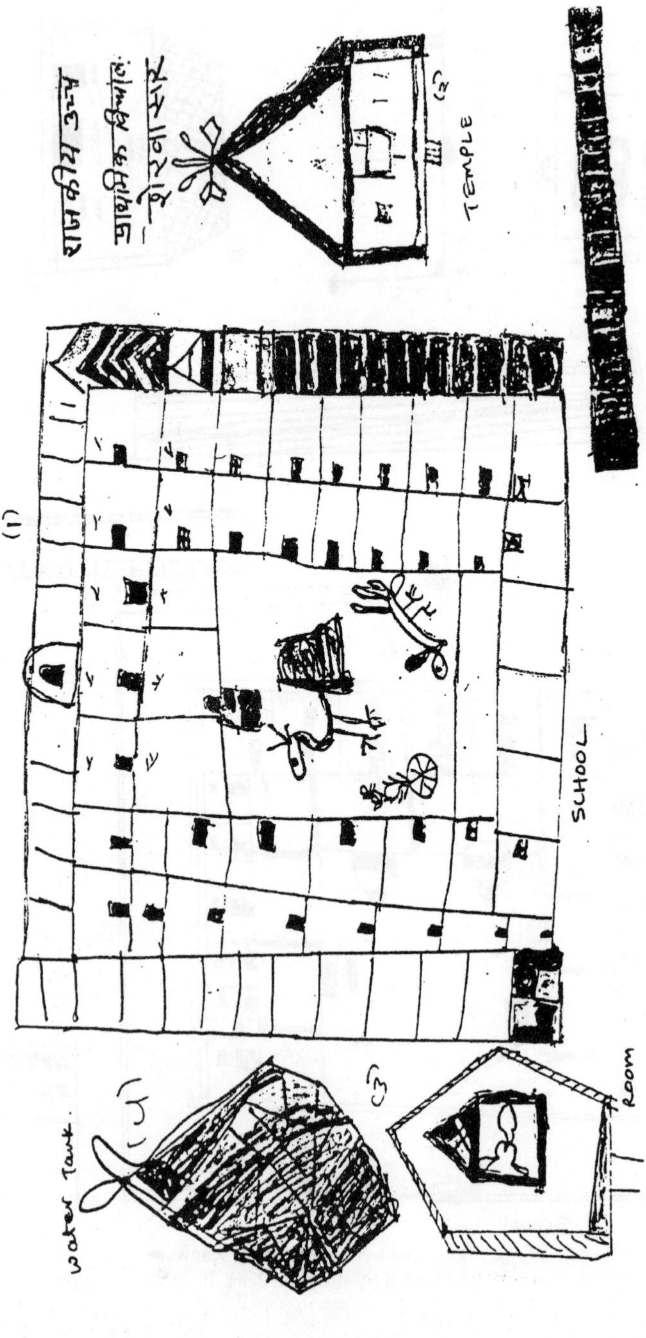

Fig. 8.3. Drawing by: Oma Kanwar
Facilitated by: Bratindi Jena

TABLE 8.2: When Asked about Secured Livelihood, boys mentioned these factors and scored it according to priority.

Boys Priority	*Scores*	*Ranks*
Bus	5	6
Road	10	1
Electricity	8	3
Tube-well (irrigation)	6	5
Water Tank	9	2
Hospital	7	4

Two drawings were common between both boys and girls, road and water tank. Road and drinking water were perceived as essential, because everyone is facing a problem on account of these. There is no road and with shifting of sand it becomes difficult to drive vehicles. No public transport wants to drive through their village because of this problem. There is no drinking water supply. There is only one water pond from where the whole village draws water. Women and children have to travel great distance to fetch water. During summer days the problem gets acute.

It is interesting to mention the difference in perceptions between the adults and children of the same village. Adults gave maximum emphasis on canal water irrigation, because that would solve their problem of crop failure in the absence of rainfall. Loaning for tractor was emphasised. The adults never perceived school education as important investment for securing livelihood. Their main focus was on economic betterment but not on social and moral betterment.

Gender Related Issues

Gender role, discrimination and related issues are quite common in the society. These are reflected during childhood. The girls participating in the drawing exercise had many real life stories to share related to the issues that they had drawn.

Manu, 10 year old said I have to bring water from the pond and fill 10 to 12 pots in the morning and about 8 pots in the evening. My brother keeps playing. He does not even go to school. Mother never asks him to fetch water. If I request him to help me he gets angry and says it is a women's job and you should do without complaining.

Oma 14 years old said I have to clean the home make tea and cook food. My brothers do only outside work like grazing livestock. My father says, if your brothers do household work it does not look nice.

Drawing by Boys

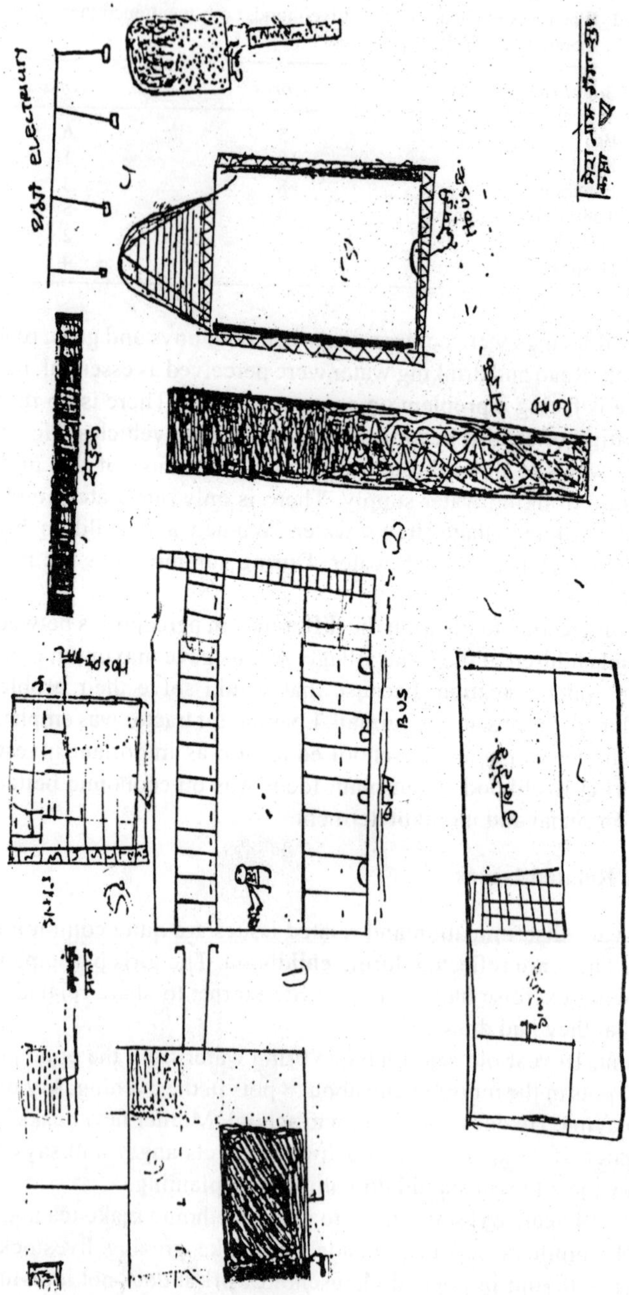

Fig. 8.4. Drawing by Mr. Ganga Suthar (Class VI)
Facilitated by: Bratindi Jena

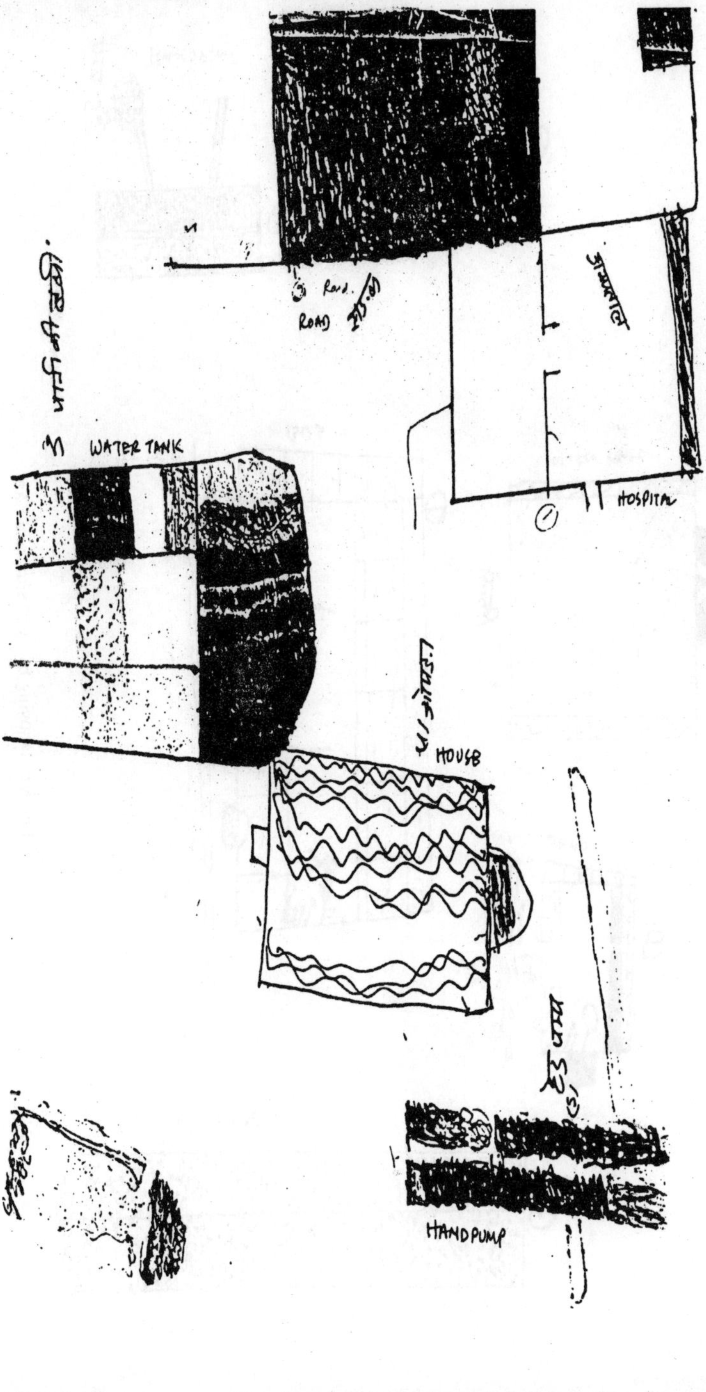

Fig. 8.5. Drawing by: Mr. Samra

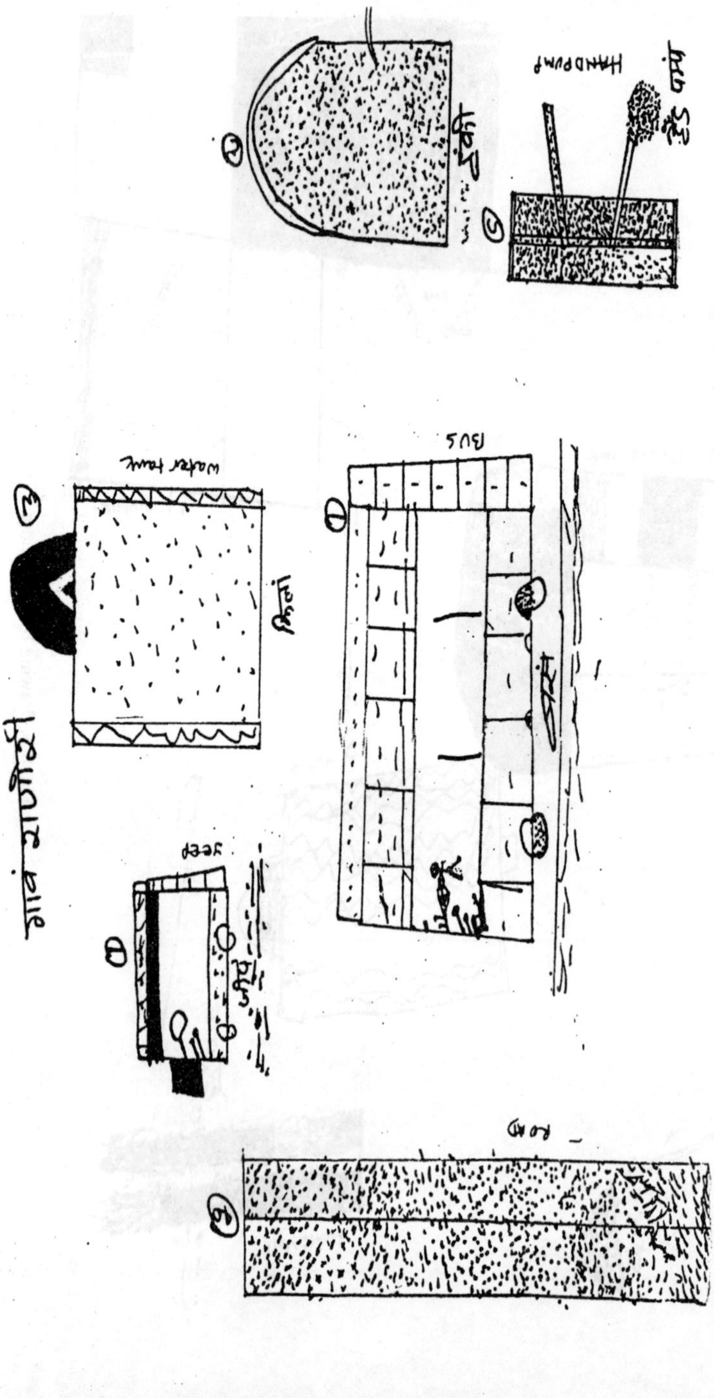

Fig. 8.6. Drawing by: Mr. Shravana Ram

My brother is forced to study but he has no interest, fails in class III. I want to go to school but my mother says I have to look after my younger brother Papu who is about seven years old.

The above are some samples of many real life incidents narrated by children. Most of them indicate the role expectations of society from childhood and girl childrens' plight in that condition. It is not that children do not understand the discrimination but they are pressurised to stick to their roles. They slowly get into those roles not by chance but by force and life goes on in that process. Children are conditioned to play gender biased role right from childhood. When discussing about different roles played by boys and girls within the household the list of activities were very clear. A girls day starts early in the morning much before a boy gets up. She has to clean the house, fetch water, milk cow, make tea, clean the cow shed, clean utensils, cook food, etc. Around mid day work for the half day gets over and after about two three hours, work for the second half starts.

Few girls study in the school. Most of them are withdrawn from the school because they have to work at home. Their marriage is fixed quite early in age and at home all say that the girl should be an expert in household chores. Since she is not going to take up any job it's no use teaching her and wasting her time.

On the contrary boys get maximum opportunity to study and get excused from household work. But very few of them utilise this opportunity. When I talked to boys about their role in the household work, they expressed clearly that often they are not allowed to do household chores and are expected to work in the field, migrate to work outside and look after livestock.

Future Expectations

In their drawings girls drew a hut or an enclosed space, a room with enough space to express themselves. Out of five girls all had drawn the picture of a hut. While probing further about the need for such a hut every child had a different purpose for drawing that space. One girl wanted to sit and study in that room because at home she was never allowed to study and was scolded for not doing household work.

Another girl wanted it as a meeting place for the group where they would be able to share their thoughts. Some one wanted to utilise it for learning new skills making drawings, toys, etc. But the fact was quite clear that out side their own home they needed a safe space for themselves, where there would have enough freedom to do whatever they wished such as rest, play, etc. Boys preferred foot ball, play ground, jeep, etc. that would make them mobile to go out of the village. Out door game was their priority.

Concluding Remarks

Childhood for a girl is short lived. While playing the role of a women the girl child loses her childhood. Although her responsibilities and her labour go unrecorded, the amount of labour a single girl contributes through the years to her home until she reaches the age of 20, estimated in terms of wages would be equivalent to Rs. 40,000 (Bhasin). The family has little or no time to listen to what they say. Very often they are considered not worth getting any attention. Even if a girl child is not well it goes unnoticed unless it's serious. For the first few days of any kind of illness she is neglected.

TABLE 8.3: Girls—What Can Bring about Development of the Village

Girls	— *Girls School* — *Lady Teacher* — *Care for Girl Child*

TABLE 8.4: Boys—What Can Bring about Development of the Village

Boys	— *Canal* — *Jeep* — *Better Road*

Children have the capacity to express themselves, in words or in drawings. They have their own way that one needs to understand with patience. If children are understood and involved n development planning it will have a lasting impact on the society. Because their planning would be more balanced on material and spiritual sides. Any work that aims at long lasting effect, needs to listen and consider the opinion of the next generation that has to carry the responsibility. Otherwise, the whole programme might fail or prove unsustainable for the next generation.

Understanding children will help in clarifying any vision of future development. It can create a healthy environment for the next generation. Children's vulnerability to exploitation would get reduced. Children's active participation will create a developed society and a better world for all.

Acknowledgement

The author wishes to thank all the children of Sekhasar Middle School, village Sekhasar, who actively participated in this exercise. Sincere thanks are due to Prof. Neela Mukherjee, for her constant moral support. Thanks are due to Prof. Susanna Davies of IDS Sussex for her kind cooperation and encouragement for working with children.

REFERENCES

Chambers, R. and Guijt, I. (1995), "PRA-five Year Later where are We Now, Forest, Trees and People," *News Letter No. 6/27.*

Dodd Robert, *Listening to Smaller Voices: Children in An Environment of Change, Action, Aid.*

Hamari Betiya, *Insaf ke Intezar Main: Kamla Bhasin*, Department of Women and Child Development, Directorate of Medicine and Health, Government of Rajasthan, Jaipur.

Sapkote, P. and Sharma, J. (1996), "Participatory Interaction with Children in Nepal," *PLA Notes*, 25 Feb.

9

PARTICIPATORY IMPACT ASSESSMENT Land and Water Management in Movai Kalan Village of Mirzapur, Uttar Pradesh

V. CH. S. BAHADUR AND KRIPA SANKAR

Methodology

The project is situated in Movai Kalan Village, Hallia Block, Mirzapur District, Uttar Pradesh, India. It is located at a distance of 45 kms. from Mirzapur on the bank of Belan River.

A participatory impact assessment of the project was undertaken. The methodology adopted for the impact assessment of the project was consultation with the beneficiary groups and individuals and using participatory tools which were followed by field visits.

The Village

The village is inhabited by Kol tribe, Schedule Caste, and other economically Backward Castes. The land holding size of these families range from 2 to 8 bigha and there were no irrigation facilities earlier. Though the village is located on the bank of a perennial river, the people were not able to utilise the water source because of their poor economic conditions. The agriculture was entirely depended on rain. As a result, the people were cultivating crops like paddy, maize in Kharif season and *kodo* in Rabi season and the crop yields were very low. But the crop returns were also not assured and crop failures were very frequent, as the rainfall is erratic and comprising of long dry spells. Under these conditions agriculture, which is the only source of livelihood for the people, neither provided foodgrains nor generated employment within the village. In lean season people migrated to near by towns and villages in search of wage employment. This was creating problems for the social and economic development of the people because such outside wage employment increased pressure on women, keeping children away from education, had negative effect on self confidence of local people and increased scope for exploitation. To address these problems providing irrigation source was the single most important solution.

The project objectives were:

1. To utilise the available natural resource in equitable manner.
2. Risk aversion of the farmers through supplementing irrigation.
3. Sustained income generation through better crop planning and landuse.
4. To reduce the migration of the farmers in search of employment.
5. To reduce the dependency on outside employment during lean periods.
6. To avoid the living hardship on women caused by the migration, non-availability of employment and non-secured family income.
7. To demonstrate the gains from community based management of natural resources.

The project activity was as follows:

A community based Lift Irrigation Scheme was initiated with the 37 families belonging to Kol tribe, Schedule caste and other economic backward castes whose land is situated as a continuous area and with in a range of 1 sq km from the water source.

A 20 H.P. mono block electric motor was installed on the bank of the Belan river which is a perennial source of water. A pipeline of 800 mts. length was laid with 160 mm diameter HDPE pipes to convey and discharge the water at ridge portion of the beneficiaries' land which is at a different elevation of 13.85 mts. from the water source, so that they can irrigate their lands through gravity flow. A motor chamber was constructed to protect the motor on the bank of the Belan river and a water distribution chamber was constructed at the delivery point of the water. People contributed in the earthwork to lay the pipeline from the motor chamber to delivery point, *i.e.*, a length of 800 mts.

The beneficiary group was motivated by the Organisation Arthik Anusandhau Vendra (AAK) and formed as Farmers' cooperative (Krishak Sahakari Samiti) to act as individual group to take over the programme and work for the development of the beneficiaries. The Krishak Sahakari Samiti employed a person for operation and maintenance of the motor. The water regulation and finances are being controlled by the beneficiaries themselves. The water is being distributed on the basis of area [*i.e.*, a beneficiary can irrigate a maximum area of 5 bigha (1.25 ha.)] and maintenance costs are being charged on the basis of time with the condition that the water requirement of the cropping pattern should be conservative, *i.e.*, there is no place for crops like sugarcane, banana, etc. The community meets regularly once in a month to discuss the matters.

Beneficiaries and Irrigated Area

The details of beneficiaries, land distribution and area irrigated were identified through participatory exercises like resource mapping, focus group discussions, land transect walk (field visit).

TABLE 9.1: Beneficiaries and Irrigated Area

	No. of beneficiaries	*Irrigated Area (bigha hectare)*	*Area irrigated per family*
Proposed	37	80 bigha (20 ha.)	2.16 bigha (0.54 ha.)
At present	35	98.75 bigha (24.68 ha.)	2.82 bigha (0.71 ha.)
Expected increase	16	80 bigha (20 ha.)	5 bigha (1.25 ha.)

At present, the total number of beneficiaries of the project are 35 families against 37 families proposed. Two families were in the beneficiary list but have not been able to receive the benefits of the project. This is due to the reason that there is a government road between the water distribution chamber of the lift irrigation system and land of these two beneficiaries. The efforts to obtain the permission from the government to break the road and lay a pipeline are being pursued so that these two families can also benefit from the project. In addition to these two families another 14 families who have land holdings on the other side of the road would be benefited from the programme bringing the total number of beneficiaries to 51, and the total land irrigated to 178.75 bigha (4468 ha.). This increase in the beneficiaries and the area irrigated is based on the capacity of the water pumping system and availability of the water.

Cropping Pattern and Yields

The PRA exercises which were utilised to understand the cropping pattern and crop returns were pie charts, participatory mapping and focus group discussions supported by case studies of individual beneficiaries.

So far the beneficiaries of the project cultivated crops in two crop seasons, *i.e.*, in Kharif and Rabi. The exercises revealed that, during the Kharif season the practice before the presence of the lift irrigation system was that the total land under cultivation was 50 bighas (123.5 ha.) by the 35 beneficiary farmers under rain fed conditions. Because of the poor soil conditions and lack of irrigation facilities the average yield was 2.1 quintals (0-3.0 quintals). This shows the risk factor in doing agriculture without irrigation facilities in the area. At present in the Kharif season the farmers are able to provide 3-4 supplement irrigation in crucial periods of water requirement resulting in average yield of 6 quintals of paddy per bigha, *i.e.*, 24 quintals per hectare. The crop returns were lower than expected due to the lack of agriculture inputs (manure, deweeding, etc.) required. The capability of the beneficiaries to afford the required agriculture inputs was not developed as this was the first crop. The net increase in cultivated area for Kharif season is 48.75 bigha, *i.e.*, 12.18 ha which was kept fallow earlier.

Kharif Crops and Returns

TABLE 9.2: Kharif Crop and Return

	Crops Cultivated	*Area Cultivated in bighas*	*Yield per bigha in Quintal*	*Total Yield in Quintal*	*Rate per Quintal*	*Value of total yield in terms of Rs.*
Earlier	Paddy	50.00	2.1	105.0	400	42,000.00
Present	Paddy	98.75	6.0	592.5	400	2.37,000.00

Rabi

During Rabi season all the beneficiaries cultivated wheat crop by providing 3-4 irrigations with the support of lift irrigation system. The earlier crops were *kodo* (cereal) and barley in 30 bighas land of the beneficiaries and the remaining land was kept fallow. The average yield of *kodo* (which was used only for consumption) was 2.4 quintals per bigha and the average yield of barley was 3 quintals per bigha. Barley was being cultivated by few farmers only in those lands occupying lower portions and with soils having better moisture retention. Presently the practice is to cultivate wheat in 98.75 bighas by 35 farmers. The average yield of wheat is 6 quintals per bigha and the range of yields is

5-8 quintals. The net increase in cultivated area for Rabi season was 68.75 bigha, *i.e.*, 17.19 hectares. The yields were less than expected because there was total electricity supply failure for a period of 25 days in the entire Hallia block. As a result the farmers were able to provide only 3-4 irrigation instead of 5 irrigations.

Rabi Crops and Returns

TABLE 9.3: Rabi Crops and Returns

	Crops Cultivated	*Area Cultivated in bighas*	*Yield per bigha in Quintal*	*Total Yield in Quintal*	*Rate per Quintal*	*Value of total yield in terms of Rs.*
Before	Kodo (cereal)	23.00	2.4	55.2	150	8,200.00
	Barley	7.00	3.0	21.0	500	10,500.00
Present	Wheat	98.75	6.0	592.5	500	3,45,625.00

The Pattern of Investment and Returns for Various Crops per Bigha of Land

A difference in the pattern of investments and returns is observed before and after the availability of the irrigation facilities amongst the beneficiaries for both the Kharif and the Rabi seasons. To get the necessary information case studies were conducted with individual

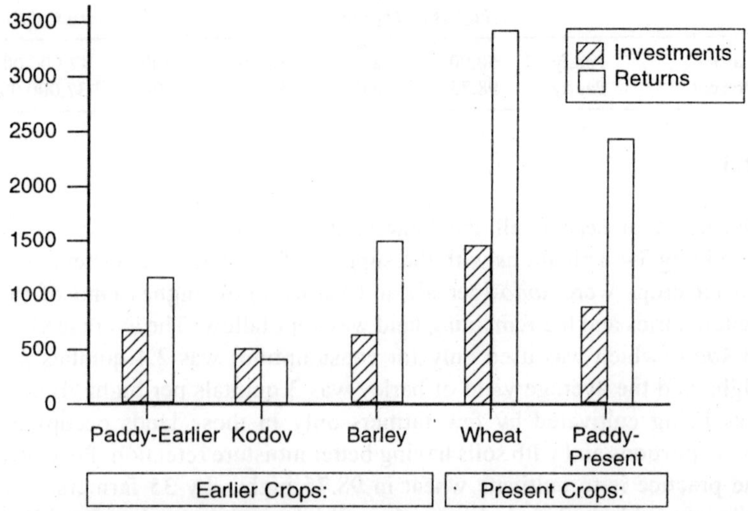

FIG. 9.1: Proportion of Investments and Returns in Agriculture (Before and Present)

farmers. Because of the abundant availability of water 7 farmers practiced vegetable cultivation in an area of 1.5 bigha out of which only one farmer did it for commercial purpose and the remaining for family requirements.

Table 9.4 provides the details of the pattern of investment and returns for various crops per bigha of land.

Paddy: The range of the yields were 0.3 quintals earlier because, the crop was entirely dependent on rain fall and there were long dry spells resulting in non-availability of water in crucial period.

At present the availability of irrigation facilities have resulted in increase in the yield to 6 quintals per bigha (the range being 5-8quintals), with only 3-4 times irrigation in spite of poor soil conditions and other agricultural inputs. This has also decreased the risk of crop failure for the farmer and assured food security.

Barley: Barley was on very limited area, which are located in the down stream portions where the soil conditions are moderately fit for moisture retention.

Kodo: Though the per bigha investments (Rs. 480) were higher than the returns (Rs. 360) for *kodo*, the farmers practiced the crop of *kodo* wherever possible as most of the investments were in kind and came from the members of the family. *Kodo* being highly tolerant to drought conditions and being a source food in periods of food shortage made the beneficiaries cultivate *kodo* crop.

Wheat: The availability of assured water resources has brought tremendous changes in the cropping pattern in Rabi season and as a result all the 35 farmers switched over to wheat cultivation which was never practiced by the beneficiaries.

Income Changes of the Beneficiaries

In order to learn about changes in the income sources of the beneficiaries with the introduction of the programme pie charts, focus group discussions and case studies of individuals were utilised. Due to non-availability of water, agriculture in one's own land was providing the least proportion of total income, *i.e.*, 8 per cent. However, presently the income from agriculture on one's own land enjoys the number one status, *i.e.*, 45 per cent of present income. The net increase in the total present income with respect to previous income is 20 per cent. The availability of water resources has also resulted in increased demand for agriculture labour within the village, thus, decreasing the extent of migration in search of work. The fact that the beneficiaries, major

TABLE 9.4: Pattern of Investment and Returns

Crop	Items of Investment	Cost of Investment item		Returns expressed as yield		Returns expressed as rupees	
		Earlier	Present	Earlier	Present	Earlier	Present
(1)	(2)	(3)	(4)	(5)	(6)	(7)	(8)
Paddy	Ploughing	160	160	3 Quintals	6	1200.00	24.00.00
(Kharif)	Seeds	125	125	per bigha	Quintal		
	Transplantation	80	80	(maximum)	range		
	Fertilizers	320	320	Range 0-3	(5-8)		
	Crop Harvesting	80	80				
	Threshing	80	80				
	Water	0	405				
Barley (Rabi)	Ploughing	160	Not	3 Quintals	—	1500.00	—
	Seeds	180	being				
	Seeds sowing	80	Practiced				
	Fertilizers	80					
	Crop Harvesting	80					
	Threshing	80					
	Water	0					
Kodo	Ploughing	160		2.4 Quintal		360.00	Not being
(Rabi)	Seeds	80					practiced
	Transplantation	—					
	Fertilizers	—					
	Crop Harvesting	80					
	Threshing	160					
	Water	—					

(Contd.)

TABLE 9.4 (*Contd.*)

(1)	(2)	(3)	(4)	(5)	(6)	(7)	(8)
Wheat (Rabi)	Ploughing	Not in	160		6		3350.00
	Seeds	Practice	180		quintal		
	Seeds sowing		80	—	1		(Rs. 3,500
	Fertilizers		280				for wheat
	Crop Harvesting		80				and Rs. 150
	Threshing		150				for the straw)
	Water		450				
Vegetables							
Lady fingers	Ploughing	Not in	360		26		13,500.00
Potato	Seeds	practice	800		quintal		
Onion	Manure		1500				
Tomato	De weeding		1000				
Brinjal	Harvesting		500				
Garlic	Water		1600				

Note: All the investments were computed at the prevailing local rates.

source of income now comes from agriculture on their own land, it has resulted in elevating the beneficiaries status from that of labourers to that of farmers. The two pie charts in Fig. 9.2 and 9.3 give the details of income sources before the availability of lift irrigation system and at present.

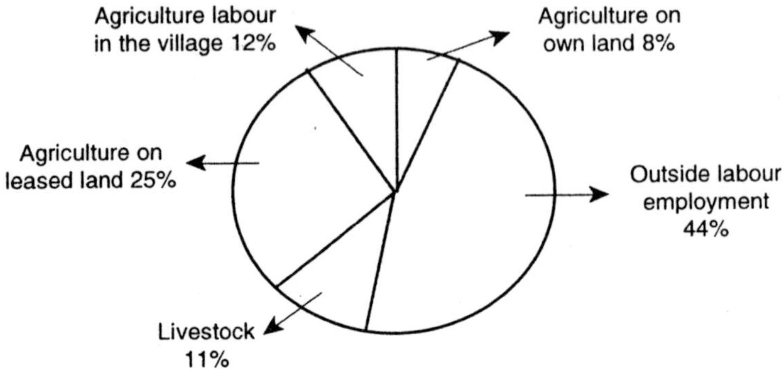

FIG. 9.2: Share of Previous Income Sources in the Village

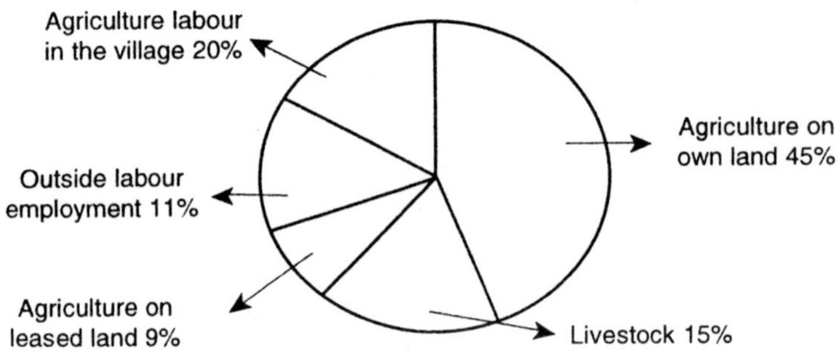

FIG. 9.3: Share of Present Income Sources in the Village

A Case Study on Change in the Sources of Income before and after the Lift Irrigation System

Mr. Bechu belongs to SC (pasi caste) and is one of the beneficiaries of the lift irrigation scheme, and had a land holding of 3 bighas. Income from cultivation on his own land amounted to Rs. 850. His major sources of income were carpet weaving and cultivation on lease land (both outside the village) amounting to Rs. 2,950 and Rs. 3,220 respectively. To undertake both these activities he had to move out of his village. Apart from those he was able to generate Rs.1,015 by way of hiring out the services of his bull and Rs. 425 through working for road repair activities. From this level Bechu moved to a position where major portion of his income now comes from tilling his own land, *i.e.*, a sum of Rs. 6,880 and the rest of his income is through carpet weaving at his house amounting to Rs. 3,200, income from cultivating one bigha of leased land is Rs. 960 and income from livestock is Rs. 3,040. Thus, his total income has gone up from Rs. 8,460 to Rs. 16,000.

Earlier Bechu was struggling to meet food requirements of the family and was under pressure in search of sources for repayment of loans. Now he is confident that he will repay the loans soon with the increased income sources.

Now Bechu does the carpet weaving at his house instead of going out. This makes the carpet weaving activity less strenuous and also does not subject himself to the pressures of the employer and is able to prevent the monotony, which comes with carpet weaving outside the village. Now he enjoys the status of a farmer rather than that of a labour who can be hired for work.

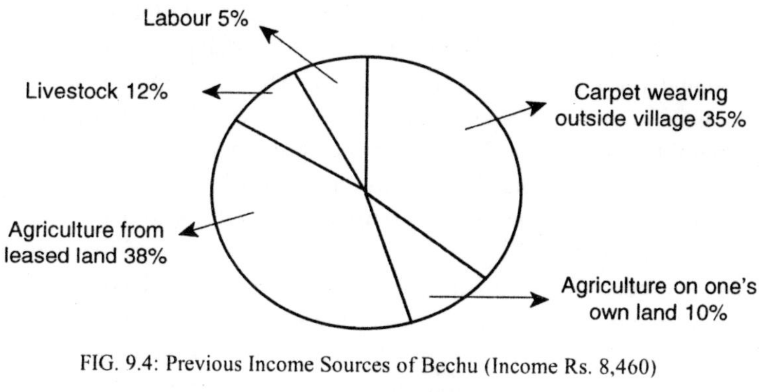

FIG. 9.4: Previous Income Sources of Bechu (Income Rs. 8,460)

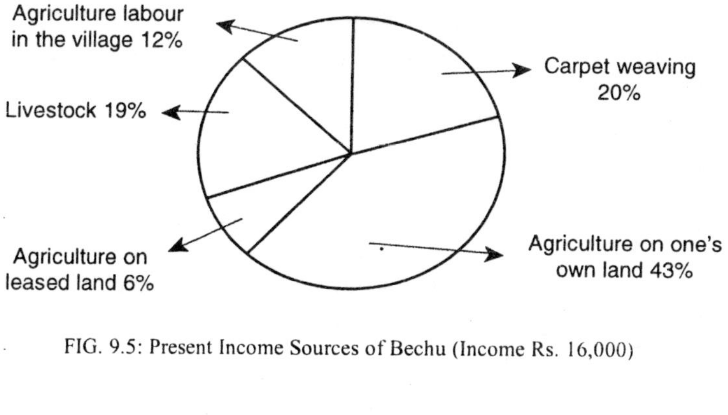

FIG. 9.5: Present Income Sources of Bechu (Income Rs. 16,000)

At present he is acting as one of the active members of the Krishak Sahakari Samiti and participating in other development activities. Now he has got opportunity to participate in social and other cultural activities where as earlier, he could hardly find time for that.

The Impact of the Lift Irrigation Scheme on Migration and Food Security

The impact on migration in search of employment and availability of foodgrains was assessed through the exercises of seasonal analysis, and focus groups discussions in Table 9.4.

Migration

Earlier 40 out of 51 beneficiary families from the village practiced migration in search of wage employment. At present only the male members of 16 families migrate in search of employment. Earlier the migration period was 10 months and at present it is for a period of 5 months. The migration of women is completely stopped, as the work is available for them in the village itself. The 16 members who have practiced migration even now are the families who have either marginal land holdings (less than 3 bigha) or the families whose lands are situated on the other side of the road and as a result unable to access water. All the 51 farmers together are stepping up their efforts to get permission from the government to take water to the other side of the road and irrigate lands of the remaining 16 beneficiaries. They have decided to take up the activity on their own if the government does not respond positively. This indicates the level of confidence of the people who are irrigating their own lands and interest of the people who are willing to be beneficiaries of the programme. Under these circumstances the possibility of water reaching the other side of the road is very strong, and the migration would be curtailed further.

Long periods of migration earlier resulted in the children of the families taking care of the livestock and house keeping and as a result get deprived of education. At present with decline in migration activities and the availability of the elder members of the family, the livestock is being looked after by the elder members of the family, women in particular. This has provided an opportunity for the children of the beneficiary families to go to school.

Availability of Foodgrains and Food Security

Earlier 20 out of 51 families were able to get foodgrains (paddy and *kodo*), from their own land for a period of 5 months. At present all the farmers who have land of at least 2 bighas and have access to water are able to get foodgrains (paddy and wheat) from their land for a period of over 10 months. The farmers who have more than 3 bighas of land have foodgrains available for all the 12 months.

Analysis of Problems before and after Implementation of the Project

To identify the impact of the project on people's problems, drawing and ranking methods of PRA were used. The other information related to changes in problems and reasons for variance was facilitated through focus group discussions. People were facilitated to identify the problems 'before' and 'after' implementation of the programme and asked to rank those problems based on the existing conditions. Then the problems were compared and reasons for variance were identified through focus group discussions.

Food Shortage and Migration

Food shortage and migration were the major problems earlier as identified by the group where as it did not show up in the list of present problems. The reasons being availability of agriculture labour with in the village due to increased area of cultivation and irrigated agriculture crops in two seasons. Though there was economic pressure on the beneficiaries for the first crop season they could manage with some support from the organisation AAK (on agreement that the loan will be returned by the end of the second crop). For the second crop people could manage themselves with the help of the returns from first crop but the loans were to be repaid and people were confident that they would do on their own from the third crop as they were getting their foodgrains from their own land.

Lack of Irrigation Facilities

Lack of irrigation facilities were identified as second major problem earlier because of the poor crop returns and crop failures which were leading to food shortage and employment opportunities. The project fulfilled the requirements of irrigation facilities. Though the project addressed the problem the reason for its emergence as third problem out of four was in consideration of the benefit of additional beneficiaries. People said that it will not be a problem by the next crop season as they have plans to access the water from the programme for additional beneficiaries.

Lack of Employment Opportunities

Lack of employment opportunities emerged as the third major problem because people were not sure of wage employment availability even out side the village. The same problem occupied last and fourth position in current analysis representing migration of the 16 people who were either not the present beneficiaries of the programme or were holding land less than 3 bigha. The women members of these families got wage employment within the village. During the discussions amongst group it was observed that problem of finding employment was negligible.

Interest on Loans

Loans at high interest which were taken in unavoidable circumstances emerged as fourth major problem. The reason was that the income of the families were being spent on food requirements as a result of which the loan obligations kept on increasing. At least 10 per cent of income earned from out side wage employment was earlier used to pay interest on loans irrespective of food requirements. There was no change in the programme as a result of which it emerged as a priority problem.

Women Migrate Out Side for Wage Labour

All the women of the existing and proposed beneficiary families were able to get agriculture labour with in the village due to the increased area of cultivation. So the problem was not shown in present set of problems.

Drinking Water Problem

Earlier there was problem of drinking water as the people were bringing water from a distance of one kilometer. The scheme is providing drinking water to some families and some families are being benefited from hand pump installed by the government. As a result there is no problem of drinking water at present.

Dowry Problem

Dowry Problem, which was not considered as a problem earlier, occupied second place in the present set of problems. This reflects the intensity of earlier problems and role of the project in addressing those problems.

Relationship between Objectives and Changes in Problems

The project addressed 5 problems out of the 6 earlier problems as prioritised by the people. This indicates the impact of the project in addressing the objectives.

(a) The resolving of problem of irrigation facilities are fulfilling the project objectives No. 1, 2 and 3.
   1. To utilise the available natural resource in equitable manner.
   2. Risk aversion of the farmers through supplement irrigation.
   3. Sustained income generation through better crop planning and landuse.

(b) The redressal of problem of food shortage and migration is fulfilling the project objectives No. 4 and 5.
   4. To reduce the migration of the farmers in search of employment.
   5. To reduce the dependency on outside employment during lean periods.

(c) The redressal of problem of migration on women is fulfilling project objectives No.6.
   6. To avoid hardship on women caused by the migration, non-availability of employment and non-secured family income.

(d) The benefits of the project and the functioning system of the Krishak Sahakari Samiti are fulfilling the project objective No.7.
   7. To demonstrate community based management of natural resources.

Social Benefits

The impact on social life of the beneficiaries was understood through focus group discussions and observations. The impact of the project on social issues was tremendous and people were experiencing the benefits of cooperation. Some of the observations were as follows:

The process of the programme developed linkages amongst the beneficiaries because it requires collective action for functioning of the system and to keep the programme alive.

The social status of Kol and SC families has been raised and they are being called as farmers where as they were earlier called as labourer.

People started working on their own land which developed the confidence of the people and reduced economic exploitation and dependency on others for employment.

With reduction in migration of the women there is reduced pressure on women in search for wage employment out side the village thereby facilitating scope for other development interventions like health education and women development programmes.

Consumption of the foodgrains were changed from *kodo* and rice to wheat and rice which was a rise in quality of life for the beneficiaries.

The beneficiaries were able to send children to schools because of reduced migration.

People started discussions on other issues like their rights and government programmes with the help of training provided by the AAK in the process of implementation of the programme.

Participation of people in the social and cultural activities of the village increased as they got opportunity to stay in the village for longer periods.

Lessons Learned

Required measures need to be taken up during the seed sowing periods so that the community follows appropriate cropping pattern keeping in view the availability of water and water requirement of crops. During planning stage of the project care should be taken in meeting the required agriculture inputs based on the economic conditions of the target group.

In the initial stages of the project implementation AAK faced many problems in bringing people together as the people were away from the village in search of employment for longer periods and people were not able to stay back due to food scarcity. Series of meetings, training programmes and exposure visits are required to involve the community in project activities for self-development.

Care should be taken to ensure land ownership of target group as there is a danger of purchasing land by outsiders and big farmers due to the irrigation facilities provided.

As a part of the infrastructure of these programmes it would be helpful if a diesel engine pumping set is also included which will support the farmers during electricity supply failures.

These programmes should be supported by some land development activities like bunding, leveling etc. which can generate employment sources as well, especially for this kind of target group. This will help in bringing people together and involve them in the implementation process as they can meet food requirements and undertake land development activities simultaneously through these programmes.

INDEX